A FASCINATING BIOGRAPHY IN WORDS, INTERVIEWS AND PHOTOGRAPHS BY STEVE CLARKE

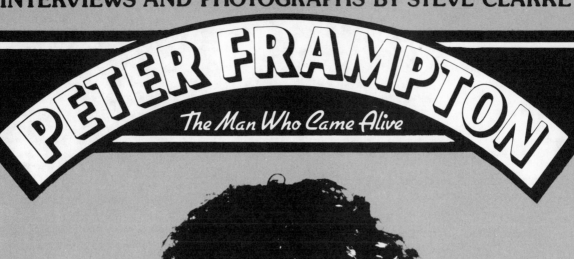

PETER FRAMPTON

The Man Who Came Alive

Contents

Few would have guessed in the mid-sixties that Peter Frampton then lead guitarist with the successful Herd, would become the overnight singing and songwriting sensation of the mid-seventies.

Frampton cast away his 'teeny-bopper' image when he joined forces with Steve Marriot in Humble Pie, a raunchy, rocking band that clambered around the top of the music tree for over four years. In those years he learnt his trade the hard way and the best way ... on the road. The rest is now history. A number one album (titled 'Frampton Comes Alive') in the U.S.A. charts for several months, hit singles plus sell-out concerts crashed Frampton to the super-star league.

Library of Congress Catalog Card Number:

Book and cover designed by Kevin Sparrow

Filmsetting by Letterbox

Front Cover Photo©Bandana 1976

A Bunch Books Package

Introduction

BY THE END OF 1976, THE LIVE DOUBLE album 'Frampton Comes Alive' had been purchased by seven million Americans and three million other record buyers worldwide. That ten million total makes it by far the best selling album of 1976 and easily the best selling double album of all time.

'Frampton Comes Alive' was released on January 30th '76 and before a month was out had made the Top Ten in the U.S.A. album charts. In March it hit the Number One position — for a solitary week. Despite competition from predictable big sellers like 'The Eagles Greatest Hits', Zeppelin's 'Presence', the Stones 'Black And Blue' and McCartney's 'Wings At The Speed of Sound', Frampton's twin set hovered in the top five for the next three months. In June it grabbed the Number One slot again and stayed there, riveted for the remainder of the summer, finally succumbing some four months later — appropriately enough — to Frampton's long standing idol, Stevie Wonder, and his 'Songs In The Key Of Life'.

One record company executive told me that during a single week of that record breaking chart marathon, 'Frampton Comes Alive' had sold a million copies. Statistics make it all sound easy, but the truth is that the groundwork had been arduous in the extreme. In the year prior to its release, Frampton had been grinding his way through the labyrinthine American rock circuit, as he had for the past three long years. Concert after concert, tour after ball-breaking tour, Frampton's intoxicating live show had built him a following across the face of America. In 1976 alone Frampton played to some two million concert-goers in the U.S.A. and still found time for a short but victorious home-coming to his native London for a three night sell-out appearance at Wembley's 10,000 seater Empire Pool. Three years earlier he had picked up barely a column inch in the British music press whilst playing support to Uriah Heep for a miserable $100 a gig.

Not surprisingly, Frampton's earnings since cracking the American market have been a cause for considerable speculation. Some observers estimate Frampton's gross income for 1976 at over 50 million dollars, a figure which upsets the remarkably unflamboyant Frampton, a young man who lives for music and little else. A more realistic appraisal might set his earnings at closer the 20 million dollar mark. One weekend, early last summer, he told me that he had earned $200,000 for appearing at just two gigs, one at Philadelphia where he played to over 100,000 fans in the city's JFK Stadium. Whatever his actual earnings were last year (and in common with most contemporary superstars, only his manager and the Inland Revenue Service will ever really know), the success of 'Frampton Comes Alive' undoubtedly means that he will want for very little for the rest of his life.

UNLIKE MANY OF HIS PEERS, FRAMPTON hasn't let success go to his head. That's a clichéd phrase, but true enough in Frampton's case. As Dee Anthony, his manager, says, he handles it so well. He remains the level-headed likeable boy from London's suburbia, who before reaching double figures had decided to dedicate himself to playing the guitar.

As an exceptionally gifted guitarist, playing with unique melody and an engaging litheness, Frampton is certainly very talented; but in purely artistic terms it's difficult to hail him as a bona fide rock heavyweight. Although he writes well and live presents an infectious mixture of rock styles always highlighted by his dazzling guitar work, it's fair to say that he has yet to prove himself an important figure in the evolution of rock.

Onstage it's a different story where, tutored by his svengali, Dee Anthony — at 50 a veteran of American show business — he establishes a rare one-to-one rapport with his fans. Unlike many of rock's other major stars, Frampton is thankfully incapable of playing the aloof macho-stud, curiously emulating instead the asexual but dynamic vitality of America's other two biggest rock acts — Elton John and Paul McCartney. With his Young-And-Pretty, Been-In-Love, Hurt-But-Now-I'm-All-Right appeal, it's easy to see why Frampton comes on to America as the idealised young Englishman. Perhaps the image is contrived, but whatever his critics may throw at him it is undeniable that Frampton consistently pleases audiences as few other artists can.

THAT BEING SAID, NO-ONE, INCLUDING Frampton, his family, his professional circle or the music industry as a whole would claim to understand the reason for his phenomenal success. In America 1976 it was almost impossible to turn on your radio without hearing one Frampton track or another and the publishers of this book were screaming for completed manuscript. Even so, I only began to suspect the real proportions of his popularity when a young fan turned to me at a concert and asked what part of the world I was from. He smiled knowingly at my reply. ''Oh yeah, England.'' A slight pause. ''Isn't that where Peter Frampton comes from?''

Chapter One

"I never wanted to be a train driver. I wanted to be the best guitar player in the world."

PETER KENNETH FRAMPTON WAS BORN AT half past six in the morning of April 20, 1950, in the predominantly middle-class township of Beckenham, Kent. When he was three the family moved from their one bedroomed flat with a leaking roof to a nearby good-sized detached house designed by an architect friend. There Peter and his younger brother Clive, grew up in a stable middle class environment on the outer reaches of the London commuter belt.

Peter's father, Owen Frampton, was fond of jazz and had played rhythm guitar in a pre-war jazz band while at London University's Goldsmiths College. He passed on his love of music to his son by giving Peter a guitar for Christmas when the boy was eight. From that time on, Peter's overriding interest in life became the guitar. 'I never wanted to be a train driver', he said. 'I wanted to be the best guitar player in the world.'

Peter's grandmother on his mother's side was 'very musical' (Peter's words) and had given her son-in-law a banjulele, a four-string hybrid of banjo and ukelele. This instrument had been collecting dust in the Framptons' attic, and as Peter grew up he continually pestered his father to fetch it down. Finally Mr. Frampton relented, and taught his son the basic chords of C, F and G on the banjulele. Initially the fledgling guitarist was content with the instrument, but after awhile he urged his father to teach him some more chords. This time the young Frampton was hooked for life, and soon transferred the four-string chords he had learnt for the banjulele to the six strings of his £4 Christmas gift, a guitar.

Peter used the talent for creative practical pursuits which he had inherited from his father to doctor the cheap guitar. He was given a pickup for his ninth birthday and with his father's help installed a tone and volume control — sophisticated work for a kid not yet into his teens. As he later told "Guitar Player Magazine", 'I'm a gadget maniac. In the early days I used to have two tape recorders. Tape recorders are like second nature to me. I love fiddling about with anything electronic. My love of gadgets and love of playing guitar went together beautifully. I used to play from after school to bedtime, sometimes five to six hours a day. I used to put down a rhythm guitar track first, and then lay down a lead, and then record that as well on another recorder. There was never an, "I'll do this to make myself better". It was just enjoyment of playing, really. I've kept quite a few of those tapes. They sound awful.'

Before a year was out Peter had made his first public appearance — at a local Boy Scout Gang Show at nearby West Wickham. The only prior clue Peter's parents had been given of their son's musical gifts came when he was an infant. Peter's mother, Peggy, claims the boy was just three when he pointed out that something was wrong with the sound coming from a piano being played in a recital broadcast on television. At the end of the programme, an announcer apologized for the piano being out of tune, explaining a sheet of music had fallen inside the instrument. She also remembers Peter's major idiosyncracy as a child: he was an imaginative story-teller. He didn't exactly lie, but it wasn't unknown for Peter to spin a few yarns to his friends using himself as the hero of these fantastic stories.

Of his childhood, Peter once told "Rave" magazine, 'I was a terrible child. Very cunning. My mother used to have to sit by me to make me go to sleep and then she'd creep out of the room, whereupon I would wake up and make her start all over again.'

THE LATE FIFTIES BRITISH POP SCENE WAS dominated by Cliff Richard and The Shadows. Richard was then a full-blooded rocker, marketed as one of Britain's answers to Elvis Presley, while The Shadows operated on two levels, as backup band for Cliff and as an entirely instrumental recording unit in their own right. Not surprisingly, the nine year-old Peter Frampton was unable to resist Cliff or The Shads (whom he'd seen on 'Oh Boy' — the day's best known TV pop show). He was particularly impressed by their lanky bespectacled lead guitarist, with the unlikely name of Hank B. Marvin.

In terms of actual playing style, Marvin's influence on rock is negligible, but as an impetus to aspiring youngsters to actually go to the trouble of obtaining an electric guitar and learning to play it (before The Shadows, electric guitars were barely heard of in Britain), Marvin is important. Musicians ranging from Eric Clapton to Neil Young have named him as an influence. Peter Frampton is no exception and when he got up at West Wickham's 1959 Gang Show it was to sing 'Travelling Light', a midtempo strumalong made famous by Cliff Richard. And when in the following year the precocious Frampton formed his own group, which he named The Trubeats, their entire set was devoted to Shadows' and Ventures' material. Later The Trubeats got into Chuck Berry and The Beatles; in fact,

15 MONTHS OLD

YEARS OLD

8 YRS

(WITH GRANNY!)

cashing in on the contemporary boom in Liverpool groups, they dubbed themselves 'The Wickham boys with the Mersey Sound'. The Trubeats had the obligatory two guitars (Frampton on lead), bass and drums line-up — although due to the cost of a drum kit there wasn't always a drummer in the group. Most likely the single biggest influence on their development was Frampton's acquiring a Hofner Club 60 Deluxe guitar (the same shape as a Les Paul), bought second-hand for £50. The cost was split in half by Frampton and his parents.

The Trubeats' gigs were restricted to scout and church halls and fetes, although in an interview with "Rave" Peter says their first gig was in a pub. 'Everybody giggled at us. I thought they were laughing because we were good, but I've since found out that it was probably because we were so diabolical. I was about 12 and the others in the group were about 16,'

he said.

The group were not without their patronage by the stars; American actor Richard Chamberlain, then known for his Dr Kildaire role, was President of The Trubeats' fan club. He had friends in the area and was persuaded by them to encourage the lads by heading the group's fan club. He even attended one of their gigs. The Trubeats weren't ignored by the local press either, as this report from 1963 shows: 'The Trubeats, although not possessing as a whole a striking personality, seem to contain all the good points of the previous acts. Their tone was varied and resonant, and they were never monotonous in their interpretations. One of the most professional numbers was 'A Taste of Honey' with the leading guitarist taking over the harmonica.'

'The leading guitarist' was of course Frampton, and apart from blowing the odd phrase on harp, Peter would often fool around with the drums during gaps in

14 YEARS OLD

13 YRS

15 YEARS OLD

rehearsals; later he would develop into a more than competent drummer.

Frampton's altogether precocious talent didn't go unnoticed by those out to make a fast buck, and various representatives of the music business started calling on the Framptons in the hope of getting their approval for Peter to go into the recording studio. Peter was 12 when these calls began and his parents insist it wasn't his looks these agents wanted to sell. But the Framptons remained resolute. They weren't going to have their son exploited. They'd agreed that Peter was going to stay at school at least until he took his 'O' levels at 16. Peter later told "New Musical Express", 'There were always people who wanted to get me away from school. It was very tempting, people saying, 'I'll make you a star.'

His father, however, did allow one of the more like-able callers to meet the band. The group were under

the impression the agent was interested in all of them. When they got wind he was only concerned with Peter's career they became jealous and Peter was promptly thrown out of the group, guitar talent or not. His father recalls, 'Peter was heartbroken by that. More so than we'll ever know. He went into limbo because all he could do then was play to himself. Peter was not particularly communicative around that age. He was very much in a world of his own. If he was at all disturbed you'd hear the crash of the front door, the clatter of his feet on the stairs and then the guitar would start. He lived for his guitar. He was a person who at that time was utterly and completely dedicated.' His mother recalls him practising between six and eight hours a day.

An account of his leaving The Trubeats which Peter gave to "Disc and Music Echo" in 1971, however, states that it was his father who took him away from the

BERT WEEDON
with his **GUILD GUITAR**

"He lived for his guitar. He was a person who at that time was utterly and completely dedicated", recalls Peter's father.

group, because he thought they were getting in the way of his school work. He said, 'Ironically it was only weeks after I left that they appeared on TV — on the talent show 'Ready Steady Win'. It hurt me to see all our fans in the audience waving banners and shouting — and another guitarist up there where I should have been.'

LEAVING THE TRUBEATS DID, HOWEVER, benefit Peter musically. There had been no record player in the house when Frampton first started playing guitar and all the pop music he heard came from television shows such as 'Oh Boy' and 'Six Five Special'. He didn't listen to the radio a lot either. It wasn't until Peter heard the Everly Brothers singing 'Till I Kissed Her' on TV that he was actually moved to go out and buy a record, even though there was nothing to play it on. His father, however, rectified the situation and bought his son a Dansette record player, then as much an essential part of a hip teenager's possessions as a decent stereo is to any rock fan today. With the Dansette, Frampton's record collection grew with a heap of Shadows and Ventures' material.

Now that he was no longer playing in a pop group, and encouraged by his father, Peter started to get into jazz and particularly jazz guitarists. His parents bought

him a Django Reinhardt album 'Django — The Unforgetable' and to this day his all-time favourite number is Reinhardt's haunting 'Nuages' ('Clouds'). His father recalls, 'He suddenly realised that what he thought were new ways of playing the guitar, Django Reinhardt had been doing all those years before.'

Frampton later told "Disc", 'I've still got the first jazz album I bought — 'Jazz for Playboys' by Kenny Burrell. I just picked it out of the pile in the record shop and of course didn't like it. But I grew with it and one of the highlights of my life was when I met him in his New York club, 'The Guitar', in October 1970 during our own tour (Humble Pie).

'Not only did I meet him, but he actually asked me to play his guitar — a priceless instrument which he's had for years and years. I eventually plucked up courage and he picked up a string bass and played with me. It was a fantastic experience. As far as the LP is concerned I've studied solo on it and I'd have asked Kenny to sign it if I'd had it with me in America.'

The importance of jazz guitarists like Reinhardt, Burrell and Wes Montgomery in moulding Peter Frampton's unique and very lyrical guitar style cannot be over-stressed. It was players like these, rather than blues and R&B guitarists — the standard influences for most first generation rock guitarists — who got through

EXTRA!

ASSEMBLY HALL
GATES GREEN ROAD CONEY HALL, WEST WICKHAM
THURSDAY 21st NOVEMBER 7.45 p.m. ONE Performance Only

BY PUBLIC DEMAND
A REPEAT PERFORMANCE

WICKHAM goes POP!
THE FABULOUS KONRADS

THE TRUBEATS

CHRISTINE CONWAY
THE CONSTREES | THE ACES

PIP AND THE BURNETTES

the psykons

MONICA TITMUSS with SHEILA PARSONS
BRIAN SHOWELL | HILDA HOLT

MUSIC IN THE MOOD

DEL & THE PANTHERS

 A WICKHAM ENTERPRISE PRESENTATION
DEVISED and PRODUCED BY DAVID M. MEYER

SEATS: 5/-, 4/- and 3/-
Bookable in advance and obtainable **NOW** from -
Harry Minting (Music), 74 Croydon Road, Coney Hall
and 137 The Avenue, West Wickham   (SPR 1587)

Poster designed by Wickham Enterprises and Printed by Hawkins & Rogers

(Above) An early taste of star billing.

to Frampton most. In the years immediately prior to his joining The Herd, Peter wouldn't listen to anything other than jazz.

He told me, 'I've listened to just about every guitarist. The ones that intrigue me more than anybody are the old jazzers, and my favourite guitarist, who's influenced me more than anybody else, is Django Reinhardt. The minute I start sounding like anybody else I go back and listen to him. But I'll never be able to play like that. I've even slowed him down on tape so I've got the riffs down really slow. And even then I can't get him. I've always listened to people I can't copy. I've never listened to blues that much. Eric Clapton turned me on, but I tried not to listen to too much of him, even though I loved his style, because everybody was copying him.

With his father's encouragement, Peter was instructed in the art of classical Spanish guitar for four years from age 10 to 14. These lessons must have done something to increase his technique as a guitarist, even though Frampton later told "Guitar Player" he hated the tuition. Frampton said, 'The main thing I learned was how to use the little finger on my left hand. I really loathed the music at the time. It was also that I hated discipline of any sort. We'd touch upon a new piece every week. I wouldn't play it until the night or 20 minutes before I went to the next lesson. Of course, I couldn't play it very well. I just wasn't interested. There were too many electric guitars floating around. And that was exciting.'

After passing his 11 plus scholarship exam, Peter attended Bromley Technical High School, where his father was head of the art department. While Peter was a first year pupil, one David Jones (né Bowie) was lounging about as a fourth former. Together with another pupil, George Underwood (later to design the front cover of Bowie's 'Hunky Dory' album), Frampton and Jones would get together in the lunch hour, meeting on the art block stairs (a natural echo chamber) to play Buddy Holly and Everly Brothers songs.

Says Peter's father, 'For his age Peter was a very mature person and mixed with the senior boys rather than the juniors.' Peter himself has said that he never had friends of his own age because he was always with his guitar, although judging from what he said to "Rave" that wasn't the only reason: 'I never got on with people of my own age. It wasn't because I was more mature than them, except musically. In every other way I was a 12 year-old, perhaps an 11 year-old. Because I wasn't ever with people of my age I didn't really grow as a person; I only progressed musically.'

Those who knew Peter with The Herd say he was shy, and Andy Bown, a member of the band and later a member of Frampton's own band, told me that Peter didn't really have the personality to carry the stardom that was thrust upon him.

Frampton was featured in an end of term concert at Bromley Tech produced in collaboration by Frampton's father and the school's music teacher. Peter formed a one-off group, a piano-guitar-drums trio called the Little Ravens; the school badge had a picture of a raven emblazened on it. According to his parents, Frampton performed the negro spiritual, 'Michael Row The Boat Ashore'. George Underwood's band, George and The Dragons with Bowie on sax, was also on the bill. Frampton was praised in the local press report of the concert as, 'Still very young, they [The Little Ravens] should do extremely well if able to continue to practice together. Peter Frampton, especially, carried a great part of the show on his diminutive shoulders . . .'.

FRAMPTON'S FATHER WAS BOWIE'S FORM master the following year and got Bowie his first job — in a design agency. His son's relationship with the future superstar was terminated, however, at the end of Peter's first year at Bromley High when Peter was transferred to Bromley Grammar.

According to his father, 'The story Peter tells about leaving because he couldn't stand calling me 'sir' isn't true. It's his stock answer. He never called me 'sir'. It was a case of atmosphere more than anything else. There were all sorts of unfortunate incidents because I was his father and it put a strain on our relationship.' One such incident occured when Peter was beaten up after school by a group of boys who didn't like his father. He told "Rave", 'When I was there I was completely bottled-up within myself, because if ever I wasn't paying attention it got straight back to my father, which the teachers thought was a great laugh. I really disliked that place. It all changed when I went to the Grammar, I made friends very easily. I was known as the bloke who played the guitar and I suppose it gave me some special sort of quality in their eyes, although I never thought about it. It was just that life would have been so boring wihout my guitar.

'I used to play at concerts at the end of term, and it was about then that I started singing, and in the third year I composed my own jazz number. I didn't join the choir because it took away practising in empty classrooms. There wasn't a day when I didn't take my guitar to school. They were very tolerant, although I think they considered me a bit of a loser because I never paid attention. I played in a group till three on Sunday nights and was dead on Mondays.'

Peter was never particularly interested in sports, particularly team games which (like his father) he despised. Gymnastics were the only sport he ever got involved with, to the extent of actually taking part in school gymnastic displays. He claims he was the first person to do a one and a half somersault at the technical school — even if he did land on his face. Frampton was far from brilliant academically. Though obviously bright, he needed a teacher to show special interest in him before he'd summon up any real interest for a school subject. He told "Rave", 'I was very nervous at school because I didn't know what was going on. They'd ask me a question and I couldn't answer it because my mind was elsewhere. Most of the teachers found it difficult to communicate with me. I liked them, though.

'I never used to get on particularly well with girls. I wasn't all that keen on them. I didn't have time, so I didn't bother. I had quite a lot of money that I earned from the group [The Trubeats] but I usually ploughed it back. I bought a tape-recorder to compose with, and I bought lots of LPs to influence my playing.'

Chapter Two

"Bach does this.
But Bach is the exception."

APART FROM THE BEATLES, THE MOST important thing happening in early Sixties British music was the R&B explosion, ultimately responsible for much of the very best rock music. Though its beginnings were developing in the Fifties, it wasn't until 1963 that a distinct R&B club scene had evolved in and around London. The Beckenham/Bromley area was not immune to the trend and some of its bands, such as Denny Mitchell and The Soundsations and The Konrads, with whom Frampton gigged but never joined, jumped onto the bandwagon. Others, like The Preachers, were formed as bona fide R&B bands.

The Preachers played Chuck Berry, Bo Diddley, Jimmy Reed and Howlin' Wolf numbers, and their trump card was their guitarist, Steve Carol. Carol was a veteran of the Fifties' rock 'n' roll scene who apparently was doing what Keith Richard did to Chuck Berry's licks before they were but a twinkle in the Rolling Stone's eye. Tragically, Carol, who is said to have looked like movie star Jack Palance, was killed in a car accident in the spring of 1964 when he and The Preachers' drummer, Tony Chapman, were driving to a gig. Chapman was hospitalised after the accident and later, out of respect for the guitarist, changed the group's name to The Herd after American Big Band leader Woody Herman's Herd.

One of those who auditioned for the vacant guitar position in the band was, according to session pianist Tim Hinkley (later to play with Alvin Lee and Steve Marriott amongst others), the then unknown Jeff Beck, arguably the most creative guitarist playing in Seventies' rock. Hinkley remembers the audition at Justin Hall in Wickham where Beck turned up with his Fender Telecaster to blow with The Preachers. The group (Hinkley maintains that for a time they were a much better band than The Stones) had been used to the Berry-derived licks Carol had let rip from his Gibson, and for them to have Beck with his more crazed Telecaster playing just wasn't on. He didn't get the gig — not because he wasn't up to scratch, but because he wasn't suitable.

Technically, Carol was replaced by one Gary Taylor, a tall, dishy blond from Streatham in South London with a deep, velvet voice. But Hinkley insists that The Herd had become a different band entirely, even if they did feature some of the same musicians; he is adamant that Carol was The Preachers' anchor. And he believes that many of the Preachers' fans stopped following The Herd, even though the band continued to play R&B.

Andy Bown was one of the musicians common to both groups. Bown was an 18 year-old arty-pretty-mod-boy,

ex-pupil of Beckenham Grammar School, who was to give up a career in advertising for a full-time one in music. Bown originally played bass with The Preachers-turned-The Herd, but after a succession of unsuitable organists had passed through the band, Bown decided to take up the instrument himself. He was the only musician from The Herd days to work with Frampton on the road and in the recording studio during the Seventies'. Bown had five years of classical piano training behind him, but had then gone in for R&B flavoured organists like Jimmy Smith and Jimmy McGriff.

IN APRIL 1965 THE PREACHERS WERE IN business again — with just the one original member, Tony Chapman and a line-up featuring Peter Frampton on guitar. The drummer hadn't heard Frampton play before, but asked him to join on the recommendation of his new organist, Peter Gosling, a refugee from The Denny Mitchell Soundsations who had seen the fourth former in action. In fact, Chapman had to promise Peter's father that Frampton, fast approaching those seemingly crucial 'O' level exams, would be home from gigs at a decent hour, so as to be up in time for school the next morning.

The Preachers' coming together was greeted in the local press with the kind of hype (or was it engineered?) which the British music press showered on Blind Faith or, more relevantly, Humble Pie in the late Sixties'. If the word supergroup had been coined in 1965, it would doubtless have been used in the local newspaper reports which greeted The Preachers' arrival on the scene, as the following demonstrates: 'A new group, The Preachers, formed to play their own kind of music, burst upon the local scene at Wickham Enterprises' Top Twenty Club marathon dance at the Justin Hall recently.

'Although expected to appeal to the more sophisticated followers of modern music, their playing was well received with enthusiasm by an audience ranging in age from 12 to 30.

'Each of The Preachers has made a name for himself as a talented performer in well-known 'pop' groups, but they have formed their own group because they wanted to play the music that specially appealed to them.'

The same line, albeit with different words, was repeated by "Beat 65", 'Kent's Top Pop Monthly'. It read, 'Here we have not so much a group, more an amalgamation of the top musicians from the North West Kent scene who have for one reason or another left the group they were playing with and have got

Spotlight on Entertainment

THE PREACHERS, a new Beckenham pop group whose first record is reviewed on Page 13, and who are to appear on the television show "Ready, Steady, Go" tonight (Friday). They are (left · to right), Peter Gosling, Peter Frampton, Ken Leamon, Tony Chapman and Pete Linton.

The Preachers, who play a combination of jazz and blues, were formed from other local groups and are led by 21-year-old Ken Leamon, an experienced jazz musician who plays alto sax, tenor sax, clarinet and flute.

They were actually founded by the drummer, 22-year-old Tony Chapman, of Thicket-road, Anerley, and 19-year-old Peter Gosling, of Upper Elmers End-road, Beckenham. Peter, who was playing the piano at the age of six, is the group's organist and main vocalist.

The bass guitarist is Peter Lynton, aged 21, and the lead guitarist, the baby of the group, is 15-year-old Peter Frampton, who is at Bromley Grammar School.

When the group first played at the Justin Hall, West Wick-ham,

(Above) 1965 cutting from a local Beckenham newspaper introducing The Preachers.

together to play the kind of music that really appeals to them'.

It sounds as though someone may have been doing a shrewd piece of hyping. "Beat 65" positively gushed about Frampton, '[he] has for some time been regarded by many, including agents and promoters, as one of the most brilliant and talented guitarists on the scene today'.

The Preachers were a five-piece guitar/bass/drums/organ/reeds outfit whose brand of R&B had more in common with that pioneered at Soho's Flamingo Club by Georgie Fame and adopted by Zoot Money's Big Roll Band and Chris Farlowe and The Thunderbirds. The original Preachers were into a more rock-orientated R&B style similar to The Stones. As time went on (and it became more fashionable), The Preachers got more into soul. Frampton himself was the featured vocalist on a couple of blues — Mose Allison's 'If You Live' and Bobby Bland's 'You're The One', as well as singing a Ray Charles number and a 'terrible piss-take [Chapman's words] of 'Wild Thing', a British hit single for The Troggs in 1966.

'Credit should also go to the 15 year-old lead guitarist, Peter Frampton. At times he looked a little bewildered by what was going on around him, but that he is both an able guitarist and an able singer is undeniable.'

Inevitably, Peter was once again surrounded by older musicians; the rest of The Preachers were in their early 20s. Chapman remembers Peter's guitar ability thus:

'He wasn't the best guitarist locally, but he had a reputation for being a very good guitarist for a young boy. He was given a lot of room to play in The Preachers. I remember one night I played him some Wes Montgomery on cans. He fell asleep while listening to it and was playing Montgomery's licks for weeks afterwards.'

CHAPMAN HAS THE DUBIOUS DISTINCTION OF being the Rolling Stones' first drummer and it was his connection with the Stones which gave The Preachers their biggest break. Born and bred in South London in 1962 he answered an ad the Stones had put in "Melody Maker" which led him to the now defunct Brewer Arms pub in Soho where the embryonic Stones were rehearsing. Chapman got the gig, he says, because he was the first drummer whose technique could master a shuffle.

Chapman was with The Stones for a year and a half, recorded an LP with them (never released) and hawked their demos around record companies. These companies, according to Chapman, universally declared a liking for the band, but suggested if they ever wanted to secure a record contract they'd have to ditch their singer.

Chapman also got Bill Wyman a job with The Stones and chipped in for the cost of Wyman's first bass. The two of them had played in several South London bands together and it was Wyman who produced The

16

Preachers only single ever released, 'Hole In My Soul' (the pun was highly intentional). They ended up promoting this single on a Rolling Stones special edition of 'Ready Steady Go', a fast-moving British TV pop programme, the likes of which British TV has unfortunately never seen since. 'Ready Steady Go' was an integral part of the mid-Sixties British pop scene, embodying the speedy groovyness which fans thought overflowed in the pop world. 'Ready Steady Go' was never dull.

On September 10, 1965, the Stones took over the entire RSG show and had as their guests, Mannfred Mann (then a fine pop-orientated R&B band who had a string of hit singles in the mid-Sixties, the first of which, '54321' was 'Ready Steady Go's' theme tune), Goldie and The Gingerbreads, an unimportant all-girl group who used the fact as a gimmick — and The Preachers. The latter were so overjoyed with the promise of a TV appearance that Chapman sent Frampton a telegram to tell him the good news. And such an event made headline news in the ''Bromley And Kentish Times''.

'Hole In My Soul' was recorded in April and released as scheduled on August 27, 1965, by which time Frampton had quit The Preachers as a full-time member because of pressures from schoolwork. Engineered by Glyn Johns, 'Hole In My Sole' (Columbia DB 7680) is a piece of jazz-flavoured R&B, the piano laying down the riff, with an over-hip lyric full of clichés. It was all uncompromising stuff and Frampton, though you wouldn't recognise him, can be heard on a brief jazzy guitar solo. Later on in the record he plays in unison with the vocalist who goes through a scat singing routine. Because of the Wyman connection, the single was reviewed in the pop weeklies. Said ''New Musical Express'', 'Preachers have a rolling piano intro in 'Hole In My Soul' which then develops into soul-type up-tempo R&B. Ear-catching solo vocal and early sax work.' ''Disc'' less complimentary: 'The Preachers try hard. Sound like Woody Allen when they speak. It's clever.' And Keith Altham, on the scene at the 'Ready Steady Go' TV studios, wrote in ''NME'', 'A hit if ever I heard one.' Wyman told the reporter, 'I don't really go out on a limb for people I record, but I really believe the group may happen.'

Both Wyman and Altham's judgement were wrong. Neither 'Hole In My Soul' or The Preachers happened, despite Wyman's patronage; he actually introduced the band on 'RSG'. The single bombed and was soon withdrawn from Columbia's catalogue.

That summer The Preachers gigged with such luminaries as Alexis Korner (regarded as father of the British R&B scene) and John Mayall's Blues Breakers. In April Tony Chapman introduced Peter to the girl he would later marry, Mary Lovett. She came from West Wickham and had a similar background to Peter's — middle class surburban. Chapman recalls, 'He was totally infatuated by her. She was really screwing him up.' Peter later told ''Disc'', 'It will sound a very corny story but it was love at first sight.' The relationship was highly respectable and the two would socialise with one another's parents. Mary, a year older than Peter, would meet the guitarist from school and they'd have tea at

their parents' houses. She says, 'Peter was very shy and sensitive — and so little. He was just really comfortable and nice. He was obviously a good person, straight-forward, honest and loyal. He was my friend and because he was a year younger than me, a lot of difference at that age, he looked up to me. He used to worry about getting ill a lot. I remember we'd go and have a Chinese meal and he'd order beans on toast because he was afraid of getting ill.'

In late 1965 The Preachers joined forces with The Other Two, whom the former had occasionally backed, and another local singer, Louis Rich, and then changed their name to The Train. The idea was Chapman's. He'd heard The Steam Packet, a London R&B band featuring Rod Stewart, Long John Baldrey and Julie Driscoll on vocals, and thought it would be a good idea to turn The Preachers into a similar operation. The Train made it onto bills at London's major R&B clubs; they gigged at Wardour Street's Flamingo where Georgie Fame was currently drawing in the emerging Mods with his very own and influential form of R&B, and they supported The Who at Brixton's Ram Jam Club — heady days for the British rock scene.

The Train's music was similar to The Preachers', but even more soul-orientated. The then Ms Attard remembers Frampton singing Len Barry's '1 2 3' — and his being terrified at the prospect. Frampton and The Other Two would provide back-up vocals for Louis Rich on a workout of T Bone Walker's classic blues, 'Stormy Monday'.

Ten days before Frampton's 16th birthday The Train recorded a single, 'Deed I Do' (MGM 1333). Once again under the studio aegis of Wyman and Jones, 'Deed I Do' was a brass-laden number with Fame-style organ, middle eight and guitar fills from Frampton that bear no resemblence to the style he was later to develop and earn his fame and fortune from. Moreover, it was a lousy composition.

It wasn't a hit. And The Train were relentlessly destined for obscurity.

BY THE TIME SUMMER 1966 CAME AROUND Peter's involvement with The Train had ceased completely. He'd taken 'O' level exams in June and had passed in English, maths, biology and music, the latter with a minimum of tuition. Of his music classes he later told ''Guitar Player'', 'Harmony was the main thing. I think it was sort of to teach you how to be the conductor of an orchestra, really. I've not yet had the opportunity or the need for using the theory I learned 'cause everything is just like a jam these days. You just shout out the chords. Harmony does help when you're doing backing vocals and learning which chords and what bass lines you can play and when it doesn't work. But I can tell by ear, anyway.

'. . . The most frustrating thing about being taught the theory of music was the fact that they used to give you a bass line and say, 'Now what we want is a tenor line, an alto line, and a soprano line on top of that.' I'd sit with the guitar or the piano at home, work it out and think, 'Wow, I've got really, really avant-garde harmonies.' I would record it, and it would sound great. But when I'd hand it in the following day, the teacher

would put a red line through it and say, 'The seventh doesn't descend. It ascends.' Then in the same breath he'd say, 'Bach does this, but Bach is the exception.' I got really annoyed that Bach was allowed to do it, but I wasn't. It was very frustrating.'

Three choices were now open to Frampton; to stay on at Bromley Grammar in the sixth form, go to a music college (something he insists would have been frustrating, and while it would have benefitted him technically, quite likely it would have taken away his feel for music), or take the plunge and become a professional pop musician.

While The Preachers and The Train floundered with their false starts, their contemporaries, The Herd, had got themselves Billy Gaff as a manager and a record contract with EMI's Parlophone label, the label for which the Beatles recorded. Gaff ran a Bromley club called The Penthouse and later formed his own management company, Gaff Management, and a less successful record label, GM Records. The former looked after The Faces, Status Quo, and Rory Gallagher, among others. Today Gaff devotes all his energies to managing Rod Stewart. In 1966 he'd produced the three singles recorded by The Herd, all nondescript mid-Sixties British pop group stuff; even the boast of a Jagger-Richard song, 'So Much In Love', couldn't push The Herd into the charts. But they had established a local reputation for themselves, as Frampton told "Rave" in 1968. 'They [The Herd] were liked by the girls and I fancied being a pop star, so I joined.' It wasn't quite that simple, and there was a fair amount of mental anguish on Frampton's part before he did become a member of The Herd.

Bown and Gaff were familiar with Peter's talent as a guitarist, having seen him play with The Preachers and The Train. When, in the summer of '66, a bust-up within the band resulted in their needing a new guitarist, it was Frampton they approached. He was very much into the idea of playing with them and gigged with The Herd during the school holidays while his parents were themselves away on holiday. When they returned, Peter had to get their go-ahead if he wanted to stay with the band on a professional basis, as he was a minor still. His parents, particularly his father with his love for anything creative, had actively encouraged

his son's musical bent from the word go. On the other hand he had always been keen that Peter's involvement in pop music shouldn't upset any potential career he might take up. And so, when in September Billy Gaff visited the Framptons to get their okay for Peter to join The Herd on a full-time basis, Peter, according to Gaff, was not expecting their reply to be an affirmative one.

Frampton was waiting at Bown's parent's house in Beckenham when Gaff called on Owen and Peggy Frampton. Gaff remembers the evening, 'I'll never forget the look of disbelief on Peter's face when I told him they'd okayed it. I assured them Peter loved music so much that if he wasn't allowed to take up music professionally he would resent his parents for the rest of his life. It must have been my indelible Irish charm.'

The manager was given 'the licence' on Peter for a year, provided (and this was his father's part of the bargain), Frampton was paid £15 a week by Gaff, more than any of the other four members of The Herd were earning. The group's line-up now read: Andy Bown (organ), Gary Taylor (rhythm guitar), Louis Cenamo (bass), Mick Underwood (drums), and Peter Frampton (guitar). Not long after, Underwood quit, and Andrew Steele, by far the group's oldest member at 26, came in on drums.

When Frampton joined The Herd, their music, according to Gaff, was 'jazz with a ballsy rock flavour.'

Two songwriters cum businessmen, Ken Howard and Alan Blaikley, were to change all that. And under their influence The Herd became for a short period one of Britain's major teenbopper attractions, boosted by the boyish good looks of Peter Frampton who Howard and Blaikley pushed to the front of the band, realizing Frampton's potential as a teen idol.

(Above) The Preachers on 'Ready Steady Go'.
(Below) Potential teen appeal personified.

Chapter Three

"Peter was a polite, well mannered young man who always looked as if he'd washed."

EVEN BEFORE HOWARD AND BLAIKLEY CAME along, The Herd had made something of a name for themselves at London's Marquee Club, the testing ground for the vast majority of British rock acts in the Sixties — once you'd established yourself at the Marquee, you invariably had a good future ahead of you. As the club's then manager John Gee puts it, 'Bands would piss themselves to get a booking at the Marquee in those days.'

In July 1966 The Herd supported The Move at the club. The Move were a Birmingham-based band who at that time were creating quite a storm among London's burgeoning underground with their psychedelic approach and an act that included breaking up TV sets and a bust of British Prime Minister, Harold Wilson. Later they had a string of classy pop hits, the earliest of which are prime examples of British psychedelic pop. Later still, The Move's Roy Wood and Carl Wayne formed the Electric Light Orchestra.

By November The Herd were topping the bill at the Marquee and had got themselves a Monday night residency. The act The Herd presented in their pre-hit singles days was, in the words of rock journalist Chris Welch, 'A mixture of cool camp and smart musicianship.' In collaboration with Andy Bown, clearly The Herd's leader and prominent performer when Frampton joined, Billy Gaff had developed an act for the group that was, for its time, altogether camp. Says Gaff, not modestly, 'The Herd were the innovators of camp rock. They'd wear dazzling, gorgeous clothes. The more outrageous we got, the more Andy like it.'

Naturally, Bown was the focal point of all this pseudo-queening and it was not unknown for the more butch elements of a Herd audience to jeer at the organist's cavortings. Preening in white gloves, Bown would walk up a while step-ladder from which he'd shower the audience with red roses. And another number, on which Bown and Gary Taylor dueted, had the two of them singing with a rose in each of their hands, a far cry from the obligatory T shirt, jeans and sneakers worn by the country's then emerging bluesmen.

Frampton's role in all this public self-flaunting was minimal. Instead, he took a back seat onstage and concentrated on playing his guitar. Says Bown, 'Peter was totally embarrassed by it.'

Gaff insists the emphasis on visual presentation didn't mean The Herd's music went to the dogs. He says before Howard and Blaikley managed the band, The Herd could hold their own musically with a set partially dedicated to jazz and blues instrumentals, including, in Gaff's opinion, a fine version of Jimmy Smith's 'Walk On The Wild Side'. Other numbers featured included Shirley Ellis's soul-orientated 'The Nitty Gritty' and The Righteous Brothers' classic Phil Spector masterpiece 'You've Lost That Loving Feeling', an ideal vehicle for Gary Taylor's rich baritone. There would also be a number of Bown's own songs.

Gaff opines, 'Howard and Blaikley made The Herd play rubbish. They turned them into just another average pop band. It didn't take a genius to realise Peter had everything. He was such an accomplished musician. I didn't fall out with Howard and Blaikley. True, they stole The Herd from me, but they'd outgrown me by then. I was as green as hell at the time.' And of Frampton himself, he says, 'Peter was a polite, well mannered young man who always looked as if he'd washed.'

Barry Saitch, The Herd's roadie, echoes Gaff's own thoughts on his disinvolvement from the band. Says Saitch, 'Although I admired him greatly, he was a bit of a bungler in those days.'

Marquee manager Gee, himself a jazz fan (a fact which influenced just whom he booked into the club), says the Marquee crowd in those days came for the music, and The Herd wouldn't have gainted their considerable following at the club if it were not for the fact they could play good music. There was, however, more to it than that. As Gee points out, 'Peter was a beautiful looking kid who hit one straight away. It was so obvious he had a tremendous charisma as a performer, even if he was totally green. And for his age, Peter's guitar solos were extremely well constructed. The Herd were a little jazz-orientated group, very musical and with all the commercial trimmings. They had a good image.'

KEN HOWARD SEES IT A LITTLE DIFFERENTLY, however. Howard had met his partner to be, Alan Blaikley, when they were both pupils at Hampstead's University College School. The two ex-public school boys re-established their friendship after they came across one another working at the BBC; Howard had graduated from Oxford and Edinburgh University and Blaikley also had an Oxford degree. Their songwriting career began inauspiciously enough in the early Sixties with a singer called Joe Grady and a song called 'The Great Train Robbery'. The record failed miserably. Howard and Blaikley's second attempt at writing a hit

single, however, paid up trumps and in 1964 they had a number one hit with The Honeycombs' 'Have I The Right', a straight-forward pop song, highly commercial but equally vacuous.

Next, Howard and Blaikley focued their abilities on Dave Dee, Dozy, Beaky, Mick and Titch, for whom they wrote ten successive top twenty hits between 1966 and 1968. The songs the two wrote for Dave Dee etc were essentially clever variations on an emphasised beat, gimmicky and highly infectious. Naturally, they were totally devoid of any artistic credibility as songs. And it's doubtful whether DDDBMT would have had the success they did without Howard and Blaikley, who also managed them, building up a viable image to sell them with. The image Dave Dee etc presented to young teenagers was flash, loud and sexy — and ultimately safe — unlike, say The Stones or The Who.

Tuned to the growing artistic awareness then emerging in pop (probably spearheaded by the Beatles' 'Rubber Soul' album released in December 1965), Howard and Blaikley began seeking artistic credibility and found The Herd after a tip-off by Steve Rowland, the record producer who worked with Dave Dee etc. Rowland had seen The Herd at the Marquee in autumn 1966 and had signed them to Double R productions, the company he ran with David Openheimer. Although Double R itself was an independent company, Rowland worked for Fontana Records (Dave Dee's label) and it was for Fontana that The Herd subsequently recorded.

Rowland and Howard and Blaikley had a 'good relationship', in Howard's words, after working together with Dave Dee etc. Rowland, according to Howard, had been told by The Herd they were looking for new management and therefore invited the two manager/songwriters down to see The Herd play at the Marquee. Howard recalls his first impressions of the band as, 'A non-denominational group with a small

following who liked to play jazz or what they called jazz. Peter was shy and retiring and he didn't move about onstage. I remember our first comment was that they haven't got an act, apart from this thing where Andy would jump down from a pair of step-ladders onto his organ.

'They wanted a commercial hit. Like every other band in those days they were desperate for recognition and success. It didn't matter how they got it, so long as they got it. They were a musical band in as much as they were playing more intricate music than most of their contemporaries. They weren't incredibly good. Peter was a reasonably good guitarist, but not a brilliant one. Andrew Steele was very competent and Andy was a good jazz organist. Louis Cenamo had just left or was in the process of going, maybe because they weren't happening.

'Peter and Gary were average musicians. Peter wasn't a very good guitarist then and I think he'd be the first to admit it. He was keen to learn. Anyone who says we neglected him as a guitarist is talking through his head. Their act was camp for those days. They were wearing some rouge. A lot of it came from the fact Gary had acne. I remember Steve saying they were rather camp. The group wanted to leave Gaff. There were things we could do for the group which he couldn't have done. There were no hard feelings between them and Billy (Bown in fact later recorded for Gaff's label). Management was something we always hated. We never wanted to do it, but if you were writing, it was necessary to control groups. We didn't think of ourselves as businessmen. We did it because we had to, for the obvious reason, to make money.

'Peter had a good appearance and charisma. The only time he came out front was when he did a Dylan number with an acoustic guitar. That got the kids really excited. He had a good bluesy, soulish quality to his voice. And we thought it wasn't a good thing having a vocalist tucked away behind an organ [ie. Bown].'

WHEN ON APRIL 14 THE HERD'S FIRST Howard and Blaikley written single, 'I Can Fly' was released, at least one of the publicity shots gave the impression that Steele, Bown and Taylor were Frampton's sidemen. And Frampton, to the displeasure of the rest of the band, particularly Bown, was the featured vocalist on 'I Can Fly', an average pop song heavily arranged (although not as heavily as the two subsequent Herd singles), which hinted at psychedelia with its characteristically decorative lyric. Howard denies that the single was a conscious attempt to cash in on the acid culture, something that was fast coming out of the closet where it had been hiding during the previous year. He says, 'I suppose it was a rather druggy song about the vibrations around at the time. The Herd weren't into drugs. They were rather well-behaved suburban boys.'

The record was greeted with favourable reviews as the following extract from "NME" demonstrates. Wrote Derek Johnson, 'Composed by Dave Dee's hit writing team, The Herd have an urgent up-tempo beat, broad harmonies and weird outer-space effects. Features the soloist in the verses, with energetic ensemble in the gimmicky chorus — plus an unusual counterharmonic interlude. Not quite so tuneful as some of Howard-Blaikley's numbers, but the performance is laden with impact. But I don't know what some of the purists will make of the title.' So confident was The Herd's agent Danny Betsch of the single's success, he bet Blaikley £100 that it would make the top three. He lost his money and 'I Can Fly' stayed firmly on the ground.

With no hit record to boost them into the bigger gig circuit (small by today's standards), The Herd continued to play clubs and colleges — and the Marquee where they were now packing them in, even attracting a few screamers. That summer The Herd were booked to play the Windsor Jazz and Blues Festival, an event organised by the Marquee's management and the precurser of the Reading Festival. The group were due to hit the stage after veteran rock 'n' roller, Jerry Lee Lewis. The rockers in the audience weren't exactly hot to see The Herd after getting themselves worked into a lather by Jerry Lee, and to prove it they hurled at the stage a scaffolding pike which landed in Steele's bass drum.

The Herd didn't go on.

It was in August that The Herd released their second Howard-Blaikley single, 'From The Underworld'. The mixture was basically the same as before, but more so. 'From The Underworld' was loaded to the gills with everything bar the proverbial kitchen sink, and to say that the arrangement is overblown is something of an understatement. The entire song smacked of pretension, with an over-elaborate lyric derived from the myth of Orpheus. Says Ken Howard, 'The record was a radical departure for us. It was something we'd been playing around with for some time. The Orpheus myth had other connotations in a modern setting — the whole underworld, criminal thing. It had nothing to do with the underground hippy thing happening at the time. We'd been taught Latin at Hampstead and some of the song's lyrics are a direct translation of Virgil.'

True, it was an ear catching sound, and the record. . . well, it lay dormant for some time before eventually cracking the charts on September 28. In fact Howard and Blaikley and the rest of those involved with The Herd had given up on the record until British DJ Alan Freeman decided to put The Herd on his 'All Systems Freeman' TV programme. It was the first time British viewers, and in particular young teenage girls, had seen Peter Frampton on TV, save for a promo clip of The Herd fooling around at an aerodrome to promote

(Left to Right) Gary Taylor, Andy Bown, Peter Frampton and Andrew Steele in an early group shot.

THE HERD

The Herd were an early attempt at artistic respectability by hit songwriters Ken Howard and Alan Blaikley after their pop successes with the Honeycombs and Dave Dee, Dozy, Beaky, Mick and Tich. Peter Frampton (vocals, guitar), Andy Bown (keyboards), Gary Taylor (bass), Andrew Steele (drums) performed their self-consciously serious songs behind an image that was the embodiment of 1968 chic. Their three hit singles which came complete with giveaway titles like 'From The Underworld' and 'Paradise Lost' (Fontana), were pretty but as pop-oriented as that of DDDBMT. Frampton soon left to form Humble Pie and the group collapsed.

The Encyclopedia of Rock

'I Can Fly' shown earlier in the year. And the reaction was staggering. As Ken Howard says, 'Peter has the kind of face which causes a reaction.'

Frampton had turned up at the Manchester TV studios where the programme was filmed in an old brown sweater, minus any kind of stage clothes, and as usual wanted to disappear into the background rather than come on as The Herd's face. To make him stand out, his managers instructed him to cut off one of the sweater's sleeves. This was done and the next day the programme was flooded with mail from viewers wanting to know where sweaters like the one Peter Frampton was wearing could be bought.

So the ball had already started rolling by the time The Herd made their debut appearance on September 28 on BBC TV's 'Top Of The Pops' (then, as now, invariably an essential stepping stone to the British charts). Inaccurately introduced by compere Jimmy Saville as 'four likely lads from Manchester', The Herd's. 'From The Underworld' was the programme's 'tip for the top' — a safe bet, seeing as how it had already charted in the lower echelons of the British charts. The record stayed in the top thirty for eight weeks, reaching number six. the Herd were featured almost continously on 'Top Of The Pops' and each week it was Howard and Blaikley's policy to ensure Frampton wore something the fans would remember him for. On one occasion he wore black pants with a white fringe stitched around his fly. Howard and Blaikley started a Herd fan club and Peter Frampton got the lion's share of the mail.

To consolidate their success, The Herd hit the road, as part of a ten day package tour featuring, would you believe, The Who, The Tremeloes (a MOR pop group with a stronger following from kids' parents than the kids themselves), and the newly formed Traffic, featuring the brilliant Steve Winwood, almost as young as Frampton himself. An eclectic bunch, to be sure. ''NME'' reporter Keith Altham was at Kingston Granada on November 3 when the tour played there — although it was during the warm-up prior to the gig that he discovered something which surprised him. Altham had interviewed The Herd several times and usually Andrew Steele, older and more cynical than the rest of the group, would rave at length about Peter Frampton's guitar playing. Altham would scoff as Steele reeled out the superlatives; after all, he'd seen The Herd at 'Top Of The Pops' and Frampton wasn't even playing his guitar. He had it slung behind his back. But after witnessing Frampton jamming the Winwood and Traffic's drummer Jim Capaldi on a jazzish piece in the deserted Kingston cinema, he realised Steele had a point and that Frampton was a musician of rare talent.

The Herd's gigs were another thing. Says Altham, 'The best things they did were before they started. They were a pop band. Occasionally the odd thing would creep out, but . . . Andy Bown was always better than people gave him credit for. Gary Taylor was an average bassist. Andrew Steele was an average drummer. One felt Peter and Gary were there strictly for their faces. The Herd were manipulated by Howard and Blaikley. I'm not knocking that. It's the way things were in those days. They could never see the wood from the trees. They could never see a band progressing

(Above & Below) The Herd publicity machine at work.

beyond their seeming limitations. If they had been shrewd they would have gradually relinquished their hold on The Herd and let them develop as a band. After all, the group were bound to be more in sympathy with their audience because of their age.

'There whole approach was encapsulated by Dave Dee. He was a projection of Howard and Blaikley's. Dave Dee's talent was in Howard and Blaikley's hands. But Peter Frampton was different and if they'd been a wider perspective they would have been able to see it.'

FRAMPTON WAS THE YOUNGEST GROUP member on the tour and not surprisingly had to cope with more than his fair share of Moon Madness — that's right, the Who's drummer Keith Moon. Bown remembers the night in Liverpool where they'd all been booked into a hotel not quite to their liking. Moon started getting his rocks off by the usual arsenal of stink bombs under doors and fireworks being let off just when a young 17 year-old like Frampton wanted to get some kip. Steele told Bown that he was off to look for another hotel for the night and the two of them left Frampton to cope with the situation as best he could. Recalls Bown, 'I don't think Peter enjoyed it very much. It was funny for a while, but then it stopped being funny. Moon never knows when to stop.'

Said Peter in ''NME'', 'There were so many different characters, from the Keith Moons of this world who blow up doors to the Stevie Winwoods and Chris Woods. But it was quite frightening for me. There were all these big groups turning up one after another.' Frampton, in fact, disobeyed doctor's orders to play the tour. He had flu.

While Bown had been ousted in favour of Frampton as The Herd's frontman by order of Howard and Blaikley, he was still well into posing, and for the tour he wore a gold suit, white silk shirt, bow tie and white shoes. But the writing was on the wall and it wasn't long before all the attention was focused on the unwilling Frampton, much to the resentment of the rest of the band.

The Herd's follow-up to 'From The Underworld', 'Paradise Lost' was put back on the release schedule due to the lengthy chart run of the former. It was released on December 1st and got to number 15 in January 1968. The formula Howard and Blaikley had worked out for The Herd was brought out again for 'Paradise Lost'. Opening with the boozy, sleazy refrain of 'The Stripper', the record was even more gimmick-ridden than the previous two — and certainly not as distinctive as its predecessor, something the public obviously realised as they gave it only a mediocre success.

Frampton's image building was about to reach its peak, however, and the media responded as a baby takes milk from its mother by dubbing Peter Frampton 'The face of '68'. After Peter narrowly escaped serious injury at a Herd gig at Streatham Ice Rink, elaborate security plans had to be made to ensure a safe exit from a gig or a TV appearance so as not to allow a repeat of the incident. At weekends a cluster of admirers would congregate outside the Framptons' home, leaving flowers and boxes of chocolates on the door step. Their son's popularity forced the Framptons to go ex-directory and Peggy Frampton spent a considerable amount of her time forging her son's signature in reply to the constant demands for Peter's autograph.

AT THE BEGINNING OF 1968 THE HERD'S ONE and only album was released. It took its title from the current 'Paradise Lost' single. Its cover was a give-away, not only the cover photograph which, naturally enough, had Frampton standing a shade forward from the others to give the impression that Bown, Steele and Taylor were his back-up musicians, but also the sleeve notes. Hype isn't the word, and Howard and Blaikley's opinion of the record-buying public must have been rock bottom to expect them to swallow the kind of drivel printed on the back of this album. It wouldn't have been so bad if it had been tongue in cheek, but Howard admits it wasn't. He says, 'One did those sort of things in those days. It's rather embarrassing, isn't it?' It certainly is.

This is what they wrote about Bown: 'A beautiful enigma. A face, a character and a voice so distinctive, once encountered, never forgotten. One of the few really original people that you meet on the pop scene,

and an organist at once sensitive and inventive. There is no easy category for Andy; he constitutes his own.' And Taylor, 'A bass man intrumentally and vocally, Gary has the sort of glamour that is given to few and worn well by even fewer. When he speaks or sings it is with the particular intensity that sends young girls and elderly matrons alike weak at the knees. A perfectionist and thinker, never at a loss for winning ideas.' And Andrew: 'Few who have seen Andrew at work would doubt that here is one of the finest drummers in any group. One would disagree with those who say he is wasted in pop. On the contrary it is typical of the quality and scope of current popular music that is contains such first-rate performers. Don't be fooled by the poker face or the languid voice; here is a born comedian, a wit of sometimes devastating accuracy, and a performer of considerable style. Also the first man in Britain to boomerang a banana.' The last line refers to part of the stage act Howard and Blaikley devised for The Herd where a bunch of bananas would rest on top of Bown's organ. During the course of their set the bananas would be thrown into the audience. In 1968 they hadn't discovered laser beams or dry ice.

And finally, this is what the sleeve note had to say about Peter: 'An angelic face, but a voice of experience that sings of loss and loneliness and love. Occasionally bobbing and weaving across the stage with the full exuberance of his seventeen years, sometimes suddenly sad and distant. Lead guitarist, occasional organist and all round musician of extraordinary promise.'

'Paradise Lost' showed The Herd as a band without any kind of direction and was a hotch-potch of the three commercial singles Howard and Blaikley had written for the group, three 'new' Howard-Blaikley numbers of no particular merit, four Bown-Frampton songs, one solo Frampton composition and an Andrew Steele number — of all things, a gospel song. Of the Bown-Frampton compositions, it was only 'Impressions Of Oliver' which stood out, the others were singularly trite and obviously the product of immature talent. Dedicated to American jazz big band leader Oliver Nelson, the track proved The Herd could play jazz and in fact they sounded more comfortable in these surroundings than in all the bogus camp, blatant commerciality and gimmickry that pervaded the rest of the album. Frampton and Bown solo impressively and Steele actually makes the piece swing.

In fact Bown, Frampton and Steele occasionally took time off from the hecticness of a Herd gig to play some music in the interval at Beckenham Jazz Club, solely for the love of playing. Frampton's own song on the album, 'On Your Own' illustrated traces of the ability he'd later develop as a writer of pretty songs, but it was nothing even remotely exceptional.

The album was more or less ignored. Steele later expressed dissatisfaction with it. He told ''NME'', 'I thought our first album would be something revolutionary — more representative of the group's individual ability, but in fact it was as non-reflective as it could be. The next one will have at least some kind of music I'll be able to identify which is us.' But there wasn't to be another Herd album and a year later in January 1969 Frampton announced he was leaving The Herd.

HERD we are again — which is almos'
pun of the ... ot quite as b
Bown's, "...
worry sir ... in my s
haven't ... h!"
rently th ... e. A
hotly pur ... i
and Gary ... d
of telling fu

What it all bo...
Andy told me as ...
he (wait for it) jo...
g in a coffee bar on...
y, is that seeing who...
l the worst jokes is hov...
e Herd pass the time on th...
y to faraway...

HOW GREAT WAS 68?

Surprises as Steve Marriott marries Jenny in '68. The Faces have numerous Chart Successes.

SCOTT WALKER - wins RAVE'S pop poll with ease; gets all his singles and L.P's in amongst the best sellers; and has his own television show. He changed his moody image into a friendlier smiling one, and is now all set to launch into the land of Hollywood and movies - his debut film surprisingly being a semi-off-beat musical!

PETER FRAMPTON - emerged as the Face of '68 and won himself fame and fortune as a prominent member of The Herd.

Chapter Four

"Darling Peter we luv you so
More than you will ever know
We think of you the whole day through
Wherever we are, whatever we do..."

TO BEGIN WITH, PETER FRAMPTON WAS amused and bewildered at becoming the idol of thousands of teenage girls. So were his parents and his girlfriend Mary. Naturally, he and the rest of The Herd had been knocked out when 'From The Underworld' hit the charts; in fact Tony Chapman, still a close friend of the group's, remembers Frampton for once in his life getting cocky when the record began to sell. The seeds of discontent, however, were there from the start of the Howard and Blaikley link-up and it wasn't long before Frampton, not yet 18, began to have certain misgivings about his new role.

Someone less sensitive or older than Frampton would probably been able to handle the situation, even relish it. But Peter, loaded with honesty and integrity, could no longer level with himself, cast as he was as a teen dream with Howard and Blaikley pulling the strings in a show he didn't want a part of anymore. He wanted to be a musician and a respected one at that, but was embarrassed at the circus in which he found himself the central performer.

The audience now turning up to see The Herd didn't give a damn whether the group's pretty, diminutive and entirely vulnerable looking guitarist could play that piece of wood and steel hanging from his adorable neck. They just wanted to scream at the kid and fantasize about him, although like his peers, in particular the Monkees' Davey Jones, and any other entirely manufactured teen idol, Frampton didn't present so much as a whiff of a threat. The adoration bestowed on the unsuspecting Frampton was, like its subject, wholesome as milk and cookies, as the following inscription on an 18th birthday card sent to Frampton from three fans shows;

> Darling Peter we luv you so
> More than you will ever know
> We think of you the whole day through
> Wherever we are, whatever we do
>
> Your face gives us courage, hope and joy
> Oh Peter you're the most wonderful boy
> That any girl could hope to meet
> At home, at school or in the street

Not the sort of stuff Mick Jagger receives in his post.

To make matters worse, Frampton wasn't only upset by being unable to attain anything like musical fulfilment with The Herd, he also was experiencing a good deal of mental anguish because he was getting all the attention to the exclusion of the others, particularly Andy Bown — not an attitude normally associated with rock stars. Explains Mary Frampton, 'Ever since I've known Peter he's always been in awe of anyone he admires and in those days he was very impressed with all of The Herd, especially Andy.' And to put the icing on this troubled cake, Andy was miffed at being ousted from the spotlight by a guy younger than himself who'd joined his band as a replacement. The Herd were not a happy band.

Recalls Ken Howard, 'There was rarely a night when there wasn't one hassle or another. They were all intelligent people with strong individual personalities. There was always one of them in a mood or on the verge of leaving — or both. Andrew Steele was the most difficult. I used to get furious because he'd bring his wife along to gigs. There'd be no communication between him and the rest of the group. And pushing Peter forward didn't go down at all well with Andy Bown. I remember him once saying, 'There's only one thing I want and that's power.' Everything was much jollier with Dave Dee.'

Howard remembers Frampton as 'a very lost, neurotic and lonely kid.' He says, 'I think he went through a very bad time. He was just a baby. He wouldn't want to go on before a gig and he'd get physically sick. He didn't want to do press interviews or any kind of promotion. He wasn't depressed all the time. He could be quite a perky fellow sometimes and he did have a sense of humour. But then all of a sudden, a terrible black depression would come over him.' Keith Altham first interviewed Peter Frampton in early 1968. He remembers him as a 'nervous, middle class kid, something of a mother's boy who seemed as if he'd been spoilt, polite and well mannered.'

The Herd, at the prompting of their management, presented to the press a united front. 'We'd have a little pep talk before an interview,' says Howard, while Bown told me The Herd were 'a publicist's dream'. Doubtless spoon fed by Howard and Blaikley, Frampton had told "NME" in October 1967, 'We have no wish to be a club band playing 'Sgt. Pepper' to a few people every night. We've tried that scene. First we want to make it as personalities. Then we'll show them what we can do as musicians.' It wasn't long before

Frampton had recovered from the initial flush of success and was more apt to speak his mind to the press. He told "NME" in December, 'Although people may regard me as a singer or the face in the group I am a skilled musician.' And from then on, interviews with Frampton would be strewn with how he wanted to be taken seriously as a musician — although when one of his colleagues was questioned by the day's pop journalist on whether the group resented Frampton's prominence in The Herd, he didn't tell the reporter what exactly was on their minds. In early '68 Gary Taylor told "NME", 'Peter has had it [the attention] all so far but then good for him. In time the others will emerge, if not as a group, then as individual personalities. I think it worries Peter more than us.' And a week later Steele had this to say to "NME", 'I cannot see that it matters because as long as Peter is with The Herd, The Herd is getting the publicity. All of us are mature enough to see that he was the immediate appeal. Also, whether you like it or not he is a very good looking guy.'

In answer to the same question in 1976, Andy Bown told me, 'Of course it bothered us.'

Occasionally, Frampton would be in such despair at the image the media had carved for him, albeit at the instigation of Howard and Blaikley, that he would be in tears. Howard and Blaikley talked the situation over with him at their Hampstead house. Says Howard, 'It was very difficult. We tried to help him. We told him this is what he wanted, that the hardest thing for a group is to get them recognised. And now The Herd had achieved that, they could do what they wanted to. We told him not to throw out the baby with the bath water. In all fairness he got cold feet.'

FRAMPTON WAS FAIRLY UNFAMILIAR WITH alcohol before he joined The Herd, though at the peak of the group's popularity he and Bown would regularly get through half a bottle of rum before going onstage. Frampton told "Rolling Stone" in 1976, 'We could never stand up too well when we were playing. All those girls screaming — they didn't know we were smashed.' The Herd didn't, however, take out their dissatisfactions by indulging in feasts of on-the-road debauchery, even though it was at that time that the rock fraternity were dipping, and sometimes saturating, their brains in acid. And to this day Frampton has never tripped.

As for Frampton's love life — well he was very much a one-girl guy. Ken Howard remembers him and Mary as inseparable. When the two went to parties, they'd sit in a corner and stare lovingly into one another's eyes. And it wasn't as if they weren't seeing enough of each other, for it was in '68 that the two moved in together, much to the displeasure of Peter's parents. Frampton had come to the conclusion he'd be happier living with Mary than with his parents, and after several terrible rows between the young folk and the Framptons, Peter and Mary ran away together. Initially they stayed at Tony Chapman's place, soon after renting a basement flat in Chiswick, West London. Peter said to "Disc" in 1971, 'That used to be such an embarrassment because it was at the peak of The Herd's success. People would

With love from
The Herd

say to me, 'What car have you got then, Rolls?' and I'd reply, 'No, an Austin 1100 actually,' and then they'd ask where I lived and I'd say a basement flat in Chiswick, and they just couldn't believe it. It was a really grotty flat.

'People always assumed that because you were high in the hit parade you were automatically wealthy — but in my case that couldn't have been further from the truth.' Originally Howard and Blaikley had paid The Herd £12 a week, which by the time of the group's third hit, 'I Don't Want Our Loving To Die' (released March 1968) had been upped to £15. On top of this their management paid for The Herd's stage clothes (bright, eye-catching threads, very much the embodiment of the Swinging London scene — long collared satin shirts, wide ties, Regency styled coats), some of their food, their hotel bills and other on-the-road overheads — and invested money in the group's equipment. Frampton's parents remember The Herd as being miserable and consistently broke. He'd give his mother £2.50 for keeping him. At the end of the week she'd invariably have to lend some of it back again so he'd be able to buy something or other — a parent subsidising her pop star son. Peter's father in fact contacted Howard and Blaikley wanting to know where all the money was going to. Owen Frampton claims Howard and Blaikley accused him of being mercenary. An accountant was duly employed to look at the manager's books — and everything was found to be in order.

'I DON'T WANT OUR LOVING TO DIE' WAS Howard and Blaikley's attempt to placate The Herd's internal troubles. By this time they realised their pushing Frampton to the front of the group was having adverse side effects. Moreover, they were fast coming to the conclusion that if they wanted to keep the band they'd have to come up with material more sympathetic to the group's original leanings towards jazz and R&B. As a result, 'I Don't Want Our Loving To Die' featured solo vocals from Bown and Taylor — as well as Frampton who, however, still sang the main body of the song. Also, it was in direct contrast to the claustrophobic pretensions of its predecessors, featuring as it did the band's musicianship without the augmentation of nigh on every session player in London. Consequently 'I Don't Want Our Loving To Die' is not only The Herd's least overblown Howard and Blaikley single, it's far and away their best, and still stands up today as a fine piece of commercial pop. Bown's organ and piano playing is featured extensively, pumping out chirping phrases on this bouyant number. What's more, the record's B side, a Bown-Frampton composition, 'Our Fairy Tale', is more of the same, showing the two had progressed as writers in the months since the release of the 'Paradise Lost' album; it's likely that if 'Our Fairy Tale' had been released as the A side, The Herd would still have had a huge hit. As it was, 'I Don't Want Our Loving To Die' gave The Herd their biggest hit, reaching the number five position in the British singles charts.

At the time Taylor told "NME", 'Anyone who thinks our new disc is a step backwards is over-hearing in my opinion. It is the biggest noise four people have ever made together and, without a grandiose orchestra, establishes the fact that we are four people and not forty four.' You don't have to be Philip Marlowe to deduce at whom that little snide was directed. Howard and Blaikley had changed their approach too late. And

before the single even charted, lawyers representing The Herd were on the phone to the two manager/songwriters saying the group wanted out.

The call didn't come as a complete surprise to Howard and Blaikley, and indeed their suspicions were confirmed when The Herd via their lawyers informed them that Andrew Oldham was going to manage them. Oldham, formerly the Rolling Stones' manager and producer, and now joint boss of the very hip Immediate Records, had befriended The Herd. He had come into contact with them through his association with the Small Faces whom he managed and who recorded for

HERD-A-WE[EK]

PETER FRAMPTON turned up for our interview 20 minutes early [rather than] being late ! His is the so-called Face Of 1968 that stares out so a[ppealingly from] book stalls and barely needs a description. Anyway, for the record the[...] eyes grey-blue, he stands 5ft. 8ins. tall and weighs a mere 8 stone 3lb. [...]

PETER FRAMPT[ON] tired of being the face of '6[8]

_____ By
NICK LOGAN

When we met he was wearing a black maxi coat over a black leather jerkin, yellow trousers and white shoes. He is a talented singer and an even more talented guitarist. But there's more to Peter Frampton than meets the eye.

It is not that he lacks personality—I found him friendly and likeable—but somewhere you sense there is more of Peter trying to surface from the public image that has been moulded around him.

Perhaps it is the fact that he has been submerged in the image conscious world of pop from a very tender age that has restricted him from developing a true personality of his own.

That could account for the fact that Peter feels he suffers from a lack of self confidence, a fault that is further tempered by a fear of being thought big-headed.

He is also getting tired of being the Face Of 1968.

" To start with I was very flattered that it should be me getting all the attention but now I am getting a bit fed up with it. At the time I thought it was a great thing but it is very hard once you get labelled like that.

Not in front

" Initially everybody wants to know about the lead singer but I don't think I am that much in front. We all have our own individual parts in the act and it is more of a group than people realise. It is not just me.

" We have all got completely different personalities and the others will come out in time."

Being so young—he will be 18 on April 22nd—I asked if he found people tried to take advantage of him. " I had found this but I think I have got over that now. I can suss people out very quickly.

" The pop business gave me a bit more confidence than I had before but there are still various occasions when I have no confidence at all. Like when I am talking t[o] anybody.

" I have a terrible trouble [with] language and sometimes [I get] tongue-tied and just canno[t...] I like meeting people but [...] when the conversation [...] I can think of nothing [...]

" An example is whe[n I went] see Jimmy McGriff at [...] and after at Rasputi[n's...] ist with the band wa[...]

I went up to h[im and shook his] hand and said [...] great.'

" Now I wa[s about the] 50th person [to say the same] thing to hi[m...] quite nice a[bout it ... said] you sonn[y...] think of [...] I sort o[f...]

" I d[...] out w[...] know[...]

RAG RAVE
GRANBY HALLS • LEICESTE[R]
FRIDAY, FEBRUARY 23rd. 8 p.m. [...]
KINKS & MO[VE]
TRAFFIC

Immediate; in fact the Faces were Immediate's most successful chart act, clocking up five hits in two years.

Although Oldham never in fact managed The Herd, Howard and Blaikley relinquished their control over the band with the minimum of litigation. After seeking management advice from the Small Faces' Steve Marriott and Ronnie Lane (the group's songwriting partnership) and Graham Nash, among others, The Herd decided to go it alone and manage themselves, although they were still contracted to Steve Rowland's Double R productions. Howard and Blaikley and The Herd, needless to say, didn't part on good terms. Group vehicles with their tyres slashed were dumped outside the group's erstwhile managers' home and in the subsequent months, particularly after Frampton quit The Herd in February 1969, there was much mud slinging from Frampton in their direction. On his departure from the group he moaned to the ''Daily Sketch'', 'I had been bought and sold like a footballer. But I never saw any of the money. The money side of it wasn't important but I was only getting £15 a week. And if you're in a pop group which makes hit records you're supposed to be getting fantastic money.'

Till this day Bown's feeling about what went down between Howard and Blaikley and The Herd are remarkably similar to those expressed by his former colleague eight years ago. He says, 'The Herd was just a mess — a load of kids running around being ripped off. It was so painful. We could have been better than the Stones. Granted the songs were excellent, especially 'Underworld', but Howard and Blaikley destroyed The Herd onstage. Musically the band weren't used to their fullest potential. They [H&B] hadn't a clue Peter could play guitar. They didn't know Andrew was one of the finest drummers around. He used to play consistently great. We were the biggest working band in Europe — the Stones weren't working at the time. I probably couldn't have explained it then but I had a gut feeling it was wrong to have someone manipulating you. I am slightly bitter about The Herd.'

Frampton's attitude towards Howard and Blaikley has understandably mellowed over the years. And he now takes the line that if it weren't for his involvement with the group he wouldn't be where he is today. The experience has, however, left its mark on him in that with the adulation bestowed on him in '76 he is extremely sensitive to becoming too much of a public property again. He will avoid places where he thinks he's going to be pestered by fans, has hired a former member of his road crew as a bodyguard who always sifts calls and callers and takes the adjacent hotel room to his own when he's on the road, and at the remotest hint of fan hysteria reaching him, Frampton takes immediate moves to prevent it from so doing. Once bitten, twice shy.

For their part Howard and Blaikley are tired of being cast as the villains of The Herd farce and regret ever managing them, saying the group's attitudes forced them to come on like school masters. Howard maintains he and his partner didn't destroy the group musically. Granted, he says, they imposed a musical direction on the band, but he insists The Herd didn't have one of their own to oppose it with. Herd roadie Barry Saitch, who ceased to work for The Herd after their split with Howard and Blaikley, agrees with Howard. He says, 'Howard and Blaikley didn't radically change The Herd onstage. The real difference they made was in the way the audiences responded.' Publicist Mac McIntyre remembers The Herd as, 'A cut above most pop bands. They were in the feel of the Move.'

Without Howard and Blaikley The Herd failed to make any substantial impression on the singles chart. Their first post-Howard and Blaikley single written by Bown and Frampton, 'Sunshine Cottage', made a brief appearance in the lowest reaches of the chart, but failed to get into the Top Twenty when it was released in October. And after 'Our Fairy Tale' it is something of an insipid disappointment.

FRAMPTON'S DECISION TO QUIT THE HERD came as a total surprise to the rest of the group. Says Bown, 'It surprised us all, especially since we'd done a single on our own and were beginning to feel our way. Peter lost his nerve but I don't blame him for it.' His decision to leave wasn't a sudden one. In July '68 Peter and Mary holidayed with Bown and Caroline in Malta. While abroad Frampton discussed with his girl-friend the idea of leaving the group. She says, 'He played around with the idea of leaving The Herd. When Peter makes a decision he listens to a lot of people and then toys around with the things which have been suggested to him before making up his mind. Once he's made up his mind, that's it and nobody can talk him out of it. I remember we felt really awful about leaving The Herd. Steve [Marriott] influenced his decision, though then there wasn't any talk of the two of them forming a group together. Steve was still with the Small Faces.' On announcing his decision to quit at the beginning of '69, Frampton explained to ''NME'', 'We tried to produce for ourselves but unfortunately it didn't work. About the same time I got fed up with the same old gigs because the music wasn't there at all.' Frampton played his last gig with The Herd at Brentwood on February 1, 1969.

The Herd released once more single before collapsing — 'The Game' in May, 1969. Frampton hadn't been replaced and the line-up was now a trio with Henry Spinetti on drums replacing Steele who'd developed TB and for health reasons had to go and live in the Channel Isles. The record wasn't a hit. And that was it, with Taylor working for a time as a dee-jay before ending up in Fox, a 70's teenybop band. Steele went on to prove his musical credibility by getting a gig with Neil Sedaka's band, where he is today. Bown has tried on two separate occasions to break through as a solo artist as well as work with Frampton's band. As I write, he's managed by Tony Chapman and is attempting to make it as a pop artist. Frampton? Well he went and got caught up with Steve Marriott, a lad who was to have a profound influence on Frampton's personality for a short time to the point where Marriott's more assertive. personality all but eclipsed the more easygoing and well mannered Beckenham boy, still suffering withdrawal symptons from being a teen idol and desperately wanting to prove his musical prowess.

Chapter Five

"I'm feeling awful cold/ I've just been bought and sold."

NO TWO WAYS ABOUT IT, THE SMALL FACES were a great group, ranking as they do alongside The Beatles, The Stones, The Kinks, Mannfred Mann and The Hollies as one of the great British singles bands of the mid-60s. Unlike The Who whose mod image was thrust upon them by their manager in order to exploit the growing cult, Small Faces were the genuine article. Their name itself was derived from mod-speak.

Formed in 1965 by guitarist Steve Marriott, a printer's son, and three other teenagers from the heart of London's East End, Ronnie Lane (bass), Jimmy Winston (organ) and Kenny Jones (drums) to play the mods' adopted music — soul and R&B — they had a hit with their first single, 'What'Cha Gonna Do About It' which got to number five in the British singles charts in September 1965. Although the song was written for them, it was in keeping with their love for black American music and possessed an earthy, teenage rawness; the riff was a direct lift from Solomon Burke's (one of the mods' main men) 'Everybody Needs Somebody To Love'. And with their initially crazed attempts to duplicate the musicianship of their 'black' idols, like the Stax house band, Booker T and the MGs (who were anyway half white), the Small Faces' energy was on a par with The Who's. Their sound was a distinctive one, marked by simple organ licks and Marriott's anarchic guitar, which together with the not supertight rhythm section of Lane and Jones formed a heady brew of chaotic raunch.

Their second single, 'I've Got Mine', from the as yet immature pens of Marriott and Lane, flopped — by which time Winston had been replaced by Ian Mc-Lagen, born and raised way across town in Hounslow. Come February '66 the group were riding high in the charts again with another raucous expression of the joys of teenagerdom, 'Sha La La La Lee', upon which the nation's mods latched in droves. For many, the Small Faces were the last word in mod sartorial elegance with their neat cropped haircuts, knitted ties, wide dark-on-light-checked shirts, a liking for jackets and pants made from either camel coloured or loud, but not garish, checked material, and a preference for suede and leather coats. The Small Faces were a natty looking combo, cocky and shot through with a warmth typical of those brought up in the tightly knit and totally unpretensious community of working class East London.

'Sha La La La Lee' was the first of nine consecutive hits the Small Faces chalked up in the next two and a half years, the following eight were all Marriott-Lane compositions. Their ability as songwriters grew considerably in a very short time, as did the group's playing skill and studio artistry. Much of the music the Small Faces recorded for Immediate (whom they joined from Decca in mid-'67) is highly inventive, as shown by singles like 'Itchycoo Park' (their only American hit and a hit the second time round in Britain when it was re-released in '76), 'Tin Soldier' and 'Lazy Sunday' demonstrate. The Small Faces were no longer just a pop group as their 1968 album 'Ogden's Nut Gone Flake' rammed home, but it was impossible for them to shake off their pop image.

While lacking the awesome stature of a 'Sgt Pepper' or a 'Pet Sounds', 'Ogden's Nut Gone Flake' is nevertheless a rock classic, even if side two doesn't live up to the excellence of side one where the group, collectively and individually, shine as musicians, vocalists, composers and arrangers. Side one of 'Ogden's Nut Gone Flake' is as good as anything the subsequent Faces (the original Small Faces minus Marriott, with Rod Stewart taking over on vocals) laid down on record, and a good deal more adventurous than anything the Faces ever did. Marriott, Lane, McLagen and Jones were obviously aware of the innovations then happening in pop, and without losing their original raunch utilised these innovations to their own advantage. 'Ogden's Nut Gone Flake' — at least side one — is an infectious fusion of the kind of soul music that had originally brought them together — psychedelia and cockney music traditions.

The record's adventurous quality spilled over to the sleeve which was round, designed to look like an Edwardian tin of Ogden's tobacco. If the record's debt to the then newly-emerged drug culture isn't apparent from the music itself, the sleeve spells it out with all the discreetness of a neon sign. Unlike The Herd, the Small Faces were into dope.

Clearly Marriott was the leader of the Small Faces although his prominence in the group didn't mean the otehr three were forgotten. As the following years would prove, Marriott's best songs were those he wrote with Ronnie Lane. But onstage it was Marriott who came over most with his aggressive attitude towards an audience. And it was Marriott who was the most frequently interviewed and photographed Small Face in the teenybop magazines. He wasn't as good looking as Frampton, but his looks had a wide eyed innocence which young girls went for. Consequently Marriott, like Frampton, had to put up with his share of teen adoration, something that began to rankle him, as he too craved for musical credibility, something unheard of from pop artistes before 1967 or at the earliest, late '66.

As well as working with pop groups, Marriott had

**The Small Faces
in their hey-day.
(Clockwise) Jones, Marriott, McLagen and Lane.**

been a child actor. When he was 12 he appeared for 18 months as the Artful Dodger in Lionel Bart's 'Oliver' and later worked in numerous TV and radio shows. He even washed dishes for a living at one point. And Marriott had left home early — at 14.

PETER FRAMPTON HAD LONG ADMIRED Marriott and the Small Faces from afar. He says, 'Steve was my original idol when he was with the Small Faces.' And like Andy Bown before, Frampton put Marriott on a pedestal. After his first meeting with Marriott, three years older than himself, Frampton was very impressed with Steve, whose experience of the world was entirely different and less sheltered than his own. He'd been wanting to meet Marriott for some time and finally called him up at his home in Marlow in the Thames valley, an hour's drive from London where Steve lived with his wife Jenny and Ronnie Lane. Frampton, accompanied by Bown, drove down to Steve's home to seek advice on who should manage The Herd after the group split from Howard and Blaikley. Bown didn't visit the Marriott household again; but Peter and his girlfriend Mary became frequent callers and a friendship developed between Frampton and Marriott. Peter and Mary were also close to Ian McLagen and his wife who lived near to their Chiswick flat.

Marriott says, 'The poor lad used to be in tears. We used to feel very sorry for him.' And he told "NME" in July 1969 (after Humble Pie's formation), 'I'd never heard him play guitar. Pete Townshend came round and said Peter Frampton was a very good guitarist. My first reaction was, 'Come off it, man.' When I heard him

play I couldn't understand why he was in such a group.' So convinced of Frampton's musical ability did Marriott become that he eventually approached McLagen, Lane and Jones with the idea of his joining the Small Faces. He thought having Frampton in the group would lessen his burden as a guitarist and would inject new blood which he thought the group was badly in need of. McLagen and Lane didn't want to know, says Marriott, because they thought Frampton was just a pretty face.

During these discussions, where Marriott acted as some kind of guru to Frampton, there was never any talk of the two forming a group together. The thought had crossed Frampton's mind, but he didn't have the nerve to put the question. Anyway Marriott never gave so much as a hint of his being anything other than happy with the Small Faces. Instead Steve suggested Peter form his own band and subsequently put him in touch with drummer Jerry Shirley and bassist Greg Ridley.

Peter, Mary and the Marriotts drove to Cambridge where Shirley lived, to check him out. Only 16, Shirley was playing with an unknown local band, Apostilic Intervention, one of the seemingly endless heavy rock groups swarming in the British rock scene. The group's name was the brainchild of Immediate boss Andrew Oldham for whom they'd recorded a couple of unsuccessful singles. At Marriott's suggestion they'd wanted to call themselves the Nice. Oldham didn't like the name. A swift change of mind on his part, however, made him decide to call P P Arnold's backing group the Nice a few weeks later. Greg Ridley, a few months younger than Marriott, had previously played with one of England's better heavy bands, Spooky Tooth who recorded for Island Records.

Peter and Mary Frampton in 1969.

When Steve Marriott became convinced of Frampton's musical ability he first attempted to include him in the Small Faces. Eventually, however, a new band began to take form — the fledgeling Humble Pie, seen rehearsing.

Through autumn '68 Frampton and Marriott's friendship blossomed. And although Marriott and Lane receive no credit on 'Sunshine Cottage' they produced the single. In October Frampton jammed with the Small Faces at Manchester's Belle Vue and just after Christmas Frampton travelled to Paris with the Small Faces to play on an album Glyn Johns was producing for French rock 'n' roll singer Johnny Halliday. It was during these sessions that Marriott finally decided he wanted to work with Frampton full-time. Peter, Mary and Johns stayed on in Paris to celebrate the new year while the Small Faces returned to London to play a gig at North London's Alexandra Palace with Joe Cocker, John Mayall and Free. The Faces had planned to close their set with a jam with Alexis Korner, widely regarded as the father of British R&B, but before they'd finished the jam Marriott walked off stage. The others didn't know what was going on. Marriott's mind was made up. He was quitting the Small Faces and on Frampton's return he immediately called him to ask if he could join his, as yet, nameless band.

Marriott told "NME" the following July, 'I had been on a bad scene the previous six months. We had been doing the same act, the same numbers we had been doing for the past five years and because we were the

Small Faces we couldn't get into other things. The numbers got stale — it was like session work. We weren't enjoying it anymore. I hope people will respect too the fact that one of the reasons I left was that I was in a rut as a teen scream. I didn't want to be a millionaire teen scream in a black Rolls Royce.' As it happened Marriott, like Frampton, was more or less broke. And one of the things he didn't tell the press concerning his break from the Small Faces was the fact he wasn't altogether pleased with Lane and McLagen's refusal to allow Frampton to join the band.

McLagen, Jones and Lane were staggered by their leader's going, but as events turned out, they went on to bigger, if not always better things, abbreviating their name to the Faces and replacing Marriott with those two rakes Ron Wood and Rod Stewart. Ironically at one point, while the group were looking for a replacement for Marriott, McLagen, finally realised Frampton's potential and wished he'd invited Frampton to join as Marriott's successor. Lane quit the Faces in 1973 for a career free from the pressures of big time rock 'n' roll, starting his own band Slim Chance, with whom he has continued to make good music, melodic and with a down-home rustic charm. The Faces themselves split in 1975 and as I write Marriott is back together with Jones

and McLagen and bassist Rick Wills who crops up later in Frampton's story.

I T SEEMED LIKE EVERY OTHER GROUP IN LATE Sixties' British rock was getting it together in the country. And just like Traffic and Blind Faith before them, Humble Pie's first extensive bout of rehearsing took place in the quiet of the English countryside. Steve Marriott had recently moved to an oak beamed cottage, complete with out buildings, in a tiny Essex village called Morton. He'd later build a studio there, but when he first moved in he rented that part of the property to Ronnie Lane. A short drive up the twisting Essex back roads from Marriott's new home brought you to another minute English village, Magdalen Laver. It was there, in the village hall, that Frampton, Marriott, Shirley and Ridley got musically acquainted with one another.

The name Humble Pie was Marriott's idea and was in keeping with the low key approach the group adopted in those early days both musically and in terms of onstage presentation. It was also indicative of how the group wanted to present itself to the world.

In these formative months Frampton's personality was heavily affected by Marriott's. He grew a beard, wore scruffy clothes and people who knew him from The Herd days were amazed to hear him talk with a cockney accent. Keith Altham, who became the group's publicist after being approached by Marriott whom he'd got to know during the Small Faces' days, remembers Frampton being subordinate to Marriott at this time. He says, 'Peter was like Steve's younger adopted brother. He tried to make himself like Steve.'

And it wasn't as if Marriott, forceful character that he undoubtedly is, wanted Peter to emulate him. Frampton's desire to adopt Steve's personality and lifestyle was probably an over-reaction to his wanting to get away from the persona forced upon him in The Herd. And not only was Marriott Peter's idol, the former Small Face was then, with his mellow, happy hippy attitude towards life, the antithesis of what Peter Frampton had been with The Herd.

Or to put it another way, Steve Marriott at this point in time was everything Peter Frampton wanted to be.

Inevitably Mary noticed the change in her boyfriend and because of what she calls Steve's disturbing influence on Peter the two split up for a brief period. 'I got fed up with the whole Humble Pie scene,' she says. Their separation didn't last more than a couple of months, but in that time Frampton moved from the basement flat the two had shared in Chiswick to a more comfortable apartment in Hampstead which Peter originally shared with Jerry Shirley. On the couple's reunion Jerry moved out and Mary moved in. She'd recently left art college and had begun to pursue a career as a model.

The change in Frampton's personality was strictly temporary and by the time Humble Pie hit the road in early September he was more like the polite, nervous, well-spoken Beckenham boy people had know from the previous years, even if Marriott continued to influence the way Frampton sang for some time to come. But as late as 1971 he bore a remarkable visual similarity to

Marriott, and as the cover of the Pie's fourth album, 'Rock On', shows, Frampton looks a deadringer for Marriott on the album's gatefold pix, right down to the cut of his moustache.

H UMBLE PIE WORKED HARD AND FAST through Spring '69 and within three months had recorded enough material for two albums — and more besides. The group signed to Andrew Oldham's Immediate label who, despite having on their books at one time or other the cream of what was then referred to as 'progressive pop', were only a few months away from financial disaster. Originally the Pie were to inaugurate an Immediate subsidiary label, Instant, but in an effort to salvage Immediate from liquidation, the band released all their recordings for Oldham on Immediate.

Oldham and his partner, Tony Calder, operated from a suite of ritzy, chandelier strewn offices in a good part of town. Oldham realised his position of power and adopted a gangster image for himself. At board room meetings those present would sit on chairs marked 1-20. Naturally Oldham pressed his butt down on chair number one. When the company moved its offices into new premises on New Oxford Street, Oldham insisted that the plaque bearing the name of the building be taken down and replaced with another on which was etched the words 'Immediate House'. The owners subsequently instructed Oldham to take his name plate down. And 'Immediate House' was no more.

Oldham and Calder would sit at a white double desk, complementing each other perfectly in Abbott and Costello double act fashion, talking in whispers — to

(Left to Right) Steve Marriott, Peter Frampton, Jerry Shirley and Greg Ridley — Humble Pie's first picture.

one another and to whoever happened to be sitting opposite. Oldham supplied the partnership's flair and had a sound knowledge of what was happening in pop. Calder was the business head.

When Oldham discussed the Humble Pie launch with Altham he told him what he wanted was front page coverage in the British music weeklies. By this time it had gradually sunk into the collective consciousness of audiences, media-persons and record company employees that pop music wasn't just something to scream at, but could in fact contain a fair degree of artistry now and then. Even so, music — however good — didn't sell entirely on its own merits (and never will) and in 1969 the image still came before the music when dealing with record sales. Oldham had to ensure Humble Pie was launched in the right way.

He put an embargo on photographers taking pictures of the band and for a time the only shots of Humble Pie available to Altham for distribution to the press were two photographs taken by top British lensmen David Bailey. In these pictures, used to promote the group's debut single, 'Natural Born Bugie', released on August 9, the group looked studiously relaxed, seated on the floor — a far cry from the stunts both The Herd and the Small Faces had performed in the past to promote themselves, yet still contrived.

The low key approach — the soft sell, if you like — extended to the cover of the group's first album, 'As Safe As Yesterday Is' released the following week with just stamp-sized snaps of the group adorning a sleeve designed to resemble a parcel.

But Oldham wanted those front pages too. And when

group — it sticks a little card on you before you start. We don't want people to think we are ego freaks who left their group to form a supergroup. We didn't.' Journalists were driven in a Rolls to these interviews, which took place at Marriott's home and the village hall where the group were rehearsing.

Apart from expressing their opposition of being called a supergroup, Humble Pie stressed how much of a democracy the Pie was and how eclectic its music was going to be, emcompassing acoustic and Indian styles (you couldn't be seen dead without clutching a sitar or a tabla if you were in a rock group in the late Sixties) as well as rock 'n' roll. Each member of the group, said Marriott, would swop instruments onstage and in the studio, and Humble Pie would strive to change their act as often as possible.

'What we're after is the enjoyment of playing,' Marriott told "NME". He explained the group's musical policy to "MM", 'An hour of electricity becomes boring . . . We want our band to be quietly powerful.' Such statements viewed in retrospect take on a distinctly ironic tone.

TO BEGIN WITH, HUMBLE PIE WERE AN entirely different backgammon game from the hard rock and subsequent heavy metal machine that was later to strike gold in America, even if the heavy rock power was always there. As Altham points out, 'My immediate reaction to Humble Pie was "no band ever played this loud". Once I got over that I realised they

the group's formation was officially announced, after months of rumours (in "Melody Maker" three months or so earlier in April), it was given maximum coverage with the front page headline proclaiming, 'Pop Giant's Supergroup', much to the displeasure of the group who spent the rest of the year living the hype down, although unlike the case of the Eric Clapton, Ginger Baker, Stevie Winwood, Rick Gretch 'supergroup' Blind Faith, it didn't backfire on them.

In July Marriott, in typical Marriott-speak, told "MM" journalist Chris Welch, 'Forget all that supergroup stuff. We're just four guys having a blow.' and 'Balls to supergroups. We're just four guys doing our best. If you want to give us a name, how about Super Looners?' He repeated himself to "NME's" Nick Logan, 'The thing that does give me the horrors however is getting out of the screaming bracket and getting landed in a supergroup bracket. Supergroup, super-

"What we're after is the enjoyment of playing" — Steve Marriott, 1969.

were very good musically.' 'Natural Born Bugie' itself was an excellent low key rock 'n' roll song very much in the feel of The Beatles' 'Get Back'. Marriott wrote the song almost as an after-thought. He had this Chuck Berry derived riff which he presented to the group early one morning in the studio and 'Natural Born Bugie' was sired from that. In terms of construction, the number wasn't as ambitious as a lot of the things the Small Faces had come up with. But its execution of a simple idea is strictly first-rate — the group playing as tight as it gets, a dirty and yet tasteful mesh of guitars and the occasional rolling piano phrase showing through ontop a crisp rhythm section. Frampton's guitar fills are uncharacteristically R&B flavored, yet portray his typical fluidity. He sings the first couple of verses by himself in a voice barely recognizable as the one which had earlier sang Howard and Blaikley's mostly pretencious lyrics. Clearly, he'd been influenced by Marriott the blues-shouter.

Lyrically, the song is laden with the stuff rock dreams are made of — sexual innuendo and references to the American south (which incidentally Marriott was yet to visit). The B side, 'Wrist Job' (an English euphemism for masturbating) was Marriott's composition again,

but this time democracy didn't prevail and the record is obviously his baby.

Humble Pie had got off to an auspicious start and despite the record's length — at over four minutes 'Bugie' wasn't likely to receive maximum radio play — charted immediately and stayed there for ten weeks, at one point reaching number five. The group were worried at their immediate success, particularly as Marriott and Frampton wanted to get away from their previous images that had been fuelled by chart success.

'As Safe As Yesterday Is' didn't, however, fulfil the promise of the single. And the album had little to recommend it. The songs were ill-formed, the playing good but marred by self indulgence, Frampton's vocals were awful, as he hopelessly tried to copy Steve, and the whole thing is sloppy. There were mitigating circumstances. The album was recorded in three weeks flat and by the time of its release was six months old. The reason for the delay was a legal wrangle between Steve Rowland's Double R Productions, with whom Frampton was still contracted, and Immediate. The dispute was settled by Immediate paying Rowland 'a substantial sum', thereby giving the all-clear for Humble Pie to release records.

Marriott didn't in fact want 'As Safe As ... ' released, but Oldham held sway. And surprisingly enough the album made a slight impression on the charts. Live, the band were entirely different from the sloppy electric hard rock raunch that was Humble Pie on 'As Safe As . . . ', and at the group's first public appearance, courageously enough in front of an invited press audience at Ronnie Scott's Club in Soho, their set started out with each member of the group doing an acoustic number — sitting crosslegged on the floor. Gradually they built up the volume to lay a few rock 'n' roll numbers on the audience. Frampton kept a very low profile, either hiding at the back of the stage behind an organ, or hardly daring to look up at the audience when he moved up front to play guitar. Marriott had no such inhibitions, or at least if he did didn't show them, coming on as aggressive and punkoid as ever.

THE BAND PLAYED THEIR FIRST GIG PROPER at a rain infested rock festival at Bilzen in Belgium with near disastrous results. They didn't get onstage until gone two in the morning and it wasn't long before the inclement weather played havoc with their instruments, putting them out of tune and at one point causing a power cut. Afterwards the group felt near suicidal. Subsequent successful gigs in Holland and Germany restored their peace of mind, however.

Humble Pie played their first British concerts in mid-October with a tour of smallish venues, including a gig

at London's Queen Elizabeth Hall. They picked up good reviews and almost everybody pointed out the excellence of Frampton's guitar playing. Their set opened with him doing a song from the soon to be released 'Town and Country' album, which Marriott had wanted released instead of 'As Safe As . . .'

'Town And Country' was thankfully a whole deal better than the Pie's first album. Throughout, Frampton's lyrical guitar embellishments stand out and while his songs lack the invention and authority of Marriott's, he had at last found a direction and the chord progressions and melody lines he introduced on this album bear a striking similarity to those he used in subsequent material. No one could deny Frampton had a good sense of melody, even if his lyrics were often embarrassingly mawkish, especially when put alongside Marriott's pithy and less personal statements.

Frampton's vocals still sounded contrived, although occasionally, as on Buddy Holly's 'Heartbeat' (the Pie wanted to do his 'Well All Right' but Blind Faith had beat them to it), his singing is more relaxed. Although it's only too apparent on 'Town And Country' Frampton and Marriott had little, if anything, in common musically; the former's penchant for light, acoustic settings establishes the feel of the album as a whole. While it isn't correct to describe 'Town And Country' as Frampton's album — because of his more mature talent and stronger personality Marriott couldn't help but dominate — for once in his life, Marriott does appear to be holding back. For instance on Jerry Shirley's 'Cold Lady' you get the feeling that if Marriott had really been himself, the music would have been a lot more powerful.

Frampton and Marriott were never to form a bona fide song writing partnership, as the latter did with Ronnie Lane, simply because there wasn't enough empathy between them, and on the album's only song where the two collaborate, together with Ridley ('Home And Away'), the song sounds like a Frampton number and not a Marriott-Frampton composition. The album was exceptionally well produced and an atmosphere of bonhomie pervades. Strangely enough it didn't chart.

In November the group, financed by Immediate, made their first appearance in America. Playing gigs mostly on the East Coast, including New York's Fillmore East, they opened up for a variety of acts, including, unappropriately enough, the Moody Blues. With the accent split between acoustic and electric material, the group, in Marriott's words, 'died on its legs'. The audience wanted high energy rock 'n' roll and Humble Pie weren't giving it to them.

On their return to England the band were greeted with the news of Immediate's imminent liquidation — rendering them short of a manager (Oldham had managed them as well as run their record company) and a recording contract. What looked like the healthiest of ongoing situations only a few months previously now seemed, to an outsider at least, like a dubious proposition. But on the inside it looked different. As Marriott told me, Humble Pie were a 'tight little family' in those days and an American tour that had bombed plus their record company going bust weren't about to take the wind out of their sails.

Chapter Six

"They both looked hungry.
Hungry for success, hungry to communicate
and hungry for food."

NORMALLY WHEN A ROCK ACT NEGOTIATES A record deal, the act's manager does it on their behalf. Very often a lawyer, the manager has more knowledge of such crucial points as money, something bands usually know more about spending than actually hussling. Humble Pie didn't do it that way at all. Although still very young boys, Frampton and Marriott had seen quite a lot of the pop scene's seamier side by this time and while each of them had experienced a far amount of success with their previous bands, neither Frampton or Marriott were rich young men.

Andrew Oldham did give them a few words of advice on how to go about securing a record deal, but when Frampton and Marriott walked into A&M Records' London St. George Street offices in late 1969 they had no manager to talk for them. What they did have was an exact figure in their heads of how much Humble Pie was worth to a record company. The amount? Some $400,000 for a five year contract during which time they were to record two albums a year. In the wake of recent record deals by Stevie Wonder and The Rolling Stones, both of whom secured million dollar sums from Motown and EMI respectively, $400,000 sounds like small fry, but as the then British head of A&M Larry Yaskiel points out, 'It was quite a large sum of money in those days.'

Yaskiel, who'd been A&M's British managing director since September of that year, was fully aware of his company's lack of home grown rock talent. And apart from releasing Joe Cocker's records in America and having a licensing deal with Island Records for their American releases, A&M were worldwide, with the likes of Sergio Mendes, the Sandpipers and the company's co-founder Herb Alpert on the label, very much an MOR slanted outfit. From an image point of view alone, Yaskiel reasoned, signing Humble Pie would be worth at least a ton. And the impression Marriott and Frampton made on him was a good one.

'They looked very tired,' he recalls. 'Peter had the gaunt good looks of an artist or a painter or a poet. They were extremely nice to talk to. Steve was a very down to earth person. Neither of them were pretenders. They were both straight forward genuine people. They both looked hungry, hungry for success, hungry to communicate and hungry for food.'

As Yaskiel found when he went to see the Pie rehearse, they had other irons in the fire. Walking into a rehearsal studio in Wardour Street where the Pie were tightening up their act, he not only heard the band's buoyant version of Ray Charles' 'Hallelujah (I Love Her So)', he also saw the record company mogul who'd signed Charles all those years ago, Atlantic Records boss Ahmet Ertegun. But Atlantic, with no credibility crisis, weren't prepared to meet the Pie's price. As A&M were, they signed the band.

With one side of their business affairs tied up, Humble Pie still had no-one to manage them. One of the names they tossed around was Chris Blackwell, founder of Island Records who'd guided the early careers of Traffic and Free among others, but he was only interested if the band were also contracted to Island Records. Another name suggested was Dee Anthony who was known to the Pie by the group's personal roadie Danny Farnham who'd previously worked for Spooky Tooth. Anthony had looked after the affairs of Spooky Tooth on their first American tour. The Pie's bassist Ridley, of course, knew Anthony too.

A meeting was arranged between the two parties and in early 1970 Humble Pie and Dee Anthony met at Park Lane's swish Inn On The Park hotel. The band played him their recently recorded, as yet unreleased album, 'Humble Pie' which they'd been working on with producer Glyn Johns at London's Olympic studios during the winter months of 1970. Anthony liked what he heard and later went to see the band play at the Marquee. Although the acoustic parts of the group's set failed to strike the chord in the audience that night at the Wardour Street club, Anthony agreed to manage Humble Pie — not only a significant event for the group as a whole, but possibly the most significant act in Frampton's career to date. For without Anthony, it's doubtful Peter Frampton would be where he is today.

The Pie were not doing as well as they ought to have done at this time. And Anthony, as he told journalist Chris Welch in "Melody Maker", saw his involvement with them as a challenge, 'They were obviously rejected by everyone. They were given a big push in America. Supergroup. And nothing happened. And I can't tell you how many people said 'you're crazy' when I took them on.'

ONE OF FIVE CHILDREN BORN TO PARENTS OF Italian extraction, Anthony was brought up in the tough neighbourhood of the Bronx in New York City. The Anthonys were a strict, close knit family in the Italian tradition. His father was a cable operator and it was the years of the Thirties' Depression which Anthony claims moulded his character. After completing war-

(Above) Dee Anthony with his protégés.

time service, where he entertained his fellow soldiers with a stand up comedy act, Anthony worked in vaudeville for a time, impersonating the likes of Al Jolson and Berry Hutton. He managed his first artiste when he was just 22, but it was working as Tony Bennett's personal roadie which gave him the out-on-the-road experience and knowledge of performer/audience communication he subsequently put to use in breaking the majority of British rock acts who emerged from the country's club scene in the late Sixties to become big money earners in the States. Anthony had a hand in the initial American success of Ten Years After, Jethro Tull, Joe Cocker, Traffic, ELP and King Crimson.

He recalled to Chris Welch, 'I learned from the boards — that's where I got my training. And I kind of incorporated that — pacing a show, contrast, why not? And today you can see it, every group is into performance and production. I used to take a personal interest in the groups and I'd see so many things wrong, and really no one was qualified to handle it and that's not belittling them, but they really didn't know what was going on in America. I worked in the band and worked in the act, and started to go for encores and reprises and all that, little showbiz schticks that used to work.'

Originally Anthony was part of International Management Combine, a company who tour-managed English bands on the road in America. Later on he formed his own company, Bandana, specifically to manage acts. Apart from Humble Pie, he also had on his books in 1970 the J Beils Band and, for a brief period, ELP. He's a close friend of Frank Barsalona who as the head of Premier Talent is America's top rock agent: apart from having knowledge of the rock business in common, the two share a compulsion for watching American TV quiz shows.

A big man — corpulent even — Anthony is indeed a King Pin and with his massive girth, extravagant Bronx accent that people so love to imitate, he comes on like a cross between Falstaff and James Cagney playing his toughest role. In a business that attracts flamboyant characters he is one of the most colourful — and most talked about. He was involved with a one-off Alvin Lee and Friends gig at London's Rainbow Theatre in the early 70s. At rehearsals he informed the musicians, 'If you blow this gig I'll kill every one of you.' While no-one believed him, remarks like that coming from Dee Anthony make them work extra hard.

Keith Altham has this to say about Anthony, 'When I first met Dee I was very suspicious of him and warned Steve [Marriott] against him. He's sharp to say the least. Now I'm a Dee Anthony fan. Other managers are either accountants, lawyers, or roadies, but Dee is a manager. You've got to have the talent but there's no doubt he made Humble Pie what they were. He broke them wide open in the States when everybody had given up on them.

'In my 15 years in the business he's the most competent manager I've come across. He fought, clawed and scratched his way up. For a guy of his age he has so much energy — a lot more than guys younger than him. He also has an amazing intellect. He's never boring and he does go on at length sometimes. He knows how to motivate an artiste.'

Larry Yaskiel puts it this way, 'I've never seen Dee Anthony show any doubts about any of his artistes in their presence and that's what basically makes him such a great man.'

THE RELEASE OF 'HUMBLE PIE' IN JULY, BY which time the band had made numerous appearances at clubs, universities and small venues in Britain, did nothing to expand their meagre British following and sold poorly in Britain. In contrast to 'Town And Country', the Humble Pie on this album were an authorative rock band, but while the group's playing and Glyn Johns' production are technically excellent, there is lacking a certain warmth, something which wasn't true of the previous Pie L.P. And much of the record sounds stilted. It's as if the passion had been bled out of the band. Perhaps they were trying too hard and taking themselves too seriously. And the best cut is not one of the hard rock tracks, but Steve Marriott's country flavoured 'Theme From Skint — See You Later Liquidator', a melodic, well arranged and produced, and featuring a great lyric which Marriott sings with total conviction. 'Theme From Skint — See You Later Liquidator' was, as its wry punning title states, a put down of certain music biz businessmen the Pie had ran into, as well as being a statement about Marriott's financial situation.

He sings in the closing bar, by which time the acoustic guitars and pedal steel have made way for Humble Pie's hard rock power, 'Mr Ridley's bought a Bentley/ Mr Oldham's sold his Rolls . . ./Mr Calder's digging holes.' Calder almost took legal action because of the song's reference to him, but when Marriott informed him he was merely singing about Calder digging holes in his garden and not digging holes for a living, he dropped the idea. Ridley had scored himself a Bentley with his share of the A&M advance. As for Marriott's being skint, unlike Frampton ('Whereas the rest of the Pie would go out and buy Lagondas, Peter would buy a Mini,' says Yaskiel), Marriott has always been on the extravagant side and in May that year he was busted to the tune of £50 for a cannabis offence which could account for the song's reference to money needed to pay for a dope fine, although the Pie were fond of eulogising dope in their songs per se.

Of 'Humble Pie's' heavy rock cuts, the best is the opening 'Live With Me', a group composition featuring

fine brooding organ from Frampton and electric piano from Marriott; the album's keyboard duties were split evenly between the two. Throughout, Frampton's guitar work has more discipline than on the previous Pie albums and had developed a hard rock edge (as the brief solo on 'Live With Me' shows) without sacrificing any of its fluidity of lyricism when a song demanded it. Though on the band written 'One Eyed Trouser — Snake Rumba' (no prizes for guessing what that refers to), an uptempo riff number, Frampton's spiralling solo seemed at odds with the rest of the music being laid down, the expensive jewel in a cheap setting.

Both the Pie and A&M, who had come to regard them very much as their baby because the band represented something of a watershed in their British operation, were disappointed with their lack of British success. Yaskiel took it personally and for a time it made him ill. He says, 'We all felt they deserved more credit than they were getting. It wasn't as if they were a lazy band. If they didn't want to work I wouldn't have minded so much. I saw how hard the band worked. They were putting it out but it wasn't coming back in. They wanted to make it badly in England.'

At the beginning of the month A&M released their first Humble Pie single, 'Big Black Dog' and to promote it A&M secured the band a spot on BBC TV's 'Top Of The Pops', the chart show Marriott and Frampton had appeared on countless times in their previous bands. Although the band didn't want to do the programme because they were still trying to live down their previous images, they agreed as a personal favour to Yaskiel to go along with it. The week before they were scheduled to actually appear on 'TOTPs', they visited the studio to trail their imminent appearance. And the Pie being the Pie, greeted the show's compere DJ Tony Blackburn in front of nine million odd viewers with their tongues firmly in their checks, each of them addressing Blackburn with the name of another well known DJ. Their humour wasn't appreciated, and not only did they fail to appear on the following week's show, the BBC refused to play 'Big Black Dog' on the radio. Yaskiel comments pointedly, 'At least the Pie were consistent in their rebellions.'

'Big Black Dog' wasn't a hit. From now on the band would spend the vast majority of its time working in America. Three years earlier Cream had discovered how lucrative (and wearing) the US tour circuit could be, and in their wake many other British bands flogged themselves around the seemingly endless stream of American venues which could provide a reasonable living for even the most minimumly talented — providing the music is loud and aggressive.

HUMBLE PIE HAD ALL THE RIGHT INGREDients to succeed on the road in America, even if they'd been suppressing them. On their return to the States later in September, Anthony gradually began to mould them into what the audience wanted and per-

(Below) Humble Pie signing for A&M Records in 1970, with attendant attorneys, accountants and presidents complete with cardboard cut-out of A&M co-owner, Herb Alpert!

Pie playing 'National Born Bugie' on English TV.

fected Steve Marriott's ability as a showman, something he became superb at. Unlike Frampton, Marriott had always been aggressive onstage and now with Anthony's guidance he turned it into an art.

From Humble Pie's beginnings, with their intentionally low key sets, when each of them had sat cross legged on the stage floor, Marriott had dominated the group's performances, albeit unintentionally. In the ensuing months he became without question the band's onstage focal point. With his introverted disposition, Frampton could hardly have challenged Marriott should he have wanted to, especially with Anthony egging Marriott on. Moreover, the longer Frampton stayed with the band the more obvious the personality differences between Frampton and Marriott became, and to a certain extent between himself and Ridley and Shirley, although in the latter's case, with his friendly easy-going personality, Shirley remained closer to Frampton than Marriott and Ridley.

B UT NOT EVERYTHING WAS HUNKY DORY with Humble Pie and the inevitable schism between Frampton and the rest of the group was growing all the time. Frampton and Marriott had started to realize the colossal differences between one another now the honeymoon period was over and the group had found its feet. It would be difficult to find two stranger bed fellows. Marriott brimful with aggressive energy, extremely extrovert, matey and hard swearing, living and playing hard while Frampton was altogether more refined, superficially weaker, but as events would prove, latently strong and with an unbridled desire to succeed, although still not quite his own man. Says Keith Altham, who dubs their coming together as 'the meeting of two impossibles': 'Peter in a way was born with a golden plectrum in his mouth. Steve was never given the same sort of benefits. Peter had to experience bad times to find himself.' Larry Yaskiel describes the difference between Marriott and Frampton as that between East End and West End.

Peter's father says the only time he's ever felt queasy about a decision his son has made was when he told him

he was getting together with Steve Marriott. He remembers, 'I said you can't have two front men. There's bound to be squabbles.' Actually, the disputes between the two weren't violent shouting matches (something Marriott probably would have preferred), Frampton would be loathe to openly disagree with anything Steve said, always wanting to get on with everyone. Instead he'd clam up. Moreover, the two had got what they needed from one another — very little in Marriott's case as Altham points out: 'Apart from the initial compromise in Humble Pie with the acoustic guitars, I don't think Steve was ever influenced by Peter. I don't think he ever turned him on to anything musically. Peter learned from Steve, not necessarily the right things, but by learning them he was able to differentiate them from the good things. Steve was a fighter. Frampton only became one later.'

While Marriott and Frampton never lost their mutual respect for each other, Frampton no longer socialized

with the rest of the group by this time. Continually on the road together in America the strain began to have its effects. Says Mary Frampton, 'He began to get very lonely with Humble Pie. He didn't have that much communication with the band and he's an introverted person anyway.'

Peter had been a vegetarian for some time and this was a source of much ribbing from the rest of the group. As Rick Wills (a friend of Jerry Shirley's from Cambridge and later to play with Frampton's Camel) says: 'They'd take the piss out of him 'cause he wouldn't eat meat. It became like a running thing in the end. They were just very insensitive to him.' And that was not all. Wills: 'Peter likes to hide away from all the

brashness that goes on in the world. He doesn't like nasty things. They were three real lads raving it up who couldn't get enough of anything. Peter couldn't cope with that and they couldn't cope with him because he wasn't the same. It was hard for them to understand why he couldn't get more involved with them 'cause he always stood apart from the band. I think he had quite a hard time of it.'

A little episode that encapsulates the difference between Frampton and Marriott, and one which illustrates both individuals' excessive characteristics, occured when the band were staying in a hotel in New York's seedy Bowery area. Steve was not at all taken with the hotel, and protesting what a khazi (British army slang for lavatory) the joint was he proceeded to pee in the wardrobe of the room where he was staying. Disgusted, Frampton left the room.

Personality differences aside, Frampton wasn't over enamoured of the band's out and out hard rock direction which he realised, with the release of a specially priced live double album that autumn, would really open the flood gates of American success for Humble Pie.

The strategy Anthony used to break Humble Pie in America was nigh on identical to that which he'd later employ to break Frampton as a solo artiste, but the Pie's success came quicker and not on such a phenomenal scale as Frampton's. Unlike Frampton, the Pie

didn't actually move to America, but they did establish a base there, rehearsing in the Capitol Theatre, Porchester in Upstate New York or holed up in some New York hotel waiting for cancellations on other people's tours so they could step in at any minute. Humble Pie were on stand-by and at first they'd play 20 minute electric sets opening for numerous other acts. Anthony almost immediately told them to ditch the acoustic material, something which didn't stand a chance of satiating the collective American rock audience's seemingly unquenchable thirst for rock 'n' roll — technically hard rock and/or heavy metal. 'Boo-gee,' demanded the audiences and the Pie delivered. They played New York's Fillmore East so often it was as if they were the theatre's house band. Yaskiel saw them there in December 1970. He recalls, 'The first gigs I saw them do were not hugely successful. Dee would be running around like a baseball coach. His armpits would be black with sweat. When a number wasn't going down well he'd signal them to cut it short and vice versa. He was like a fifth member of the band.'

By Spring 1971 the Pie had established a bona fide American following moving up the bill to the 'pocket position' (that is, if there were three acts playing, the Pie would go on second) for artistes like Edgar Winter and Alice Cooper at the bigger venues. Dee Anthony's policy of 'hit and run' was already working.

In March the band's fourth album, 'Rock On' (the title itself a statement of their new found policy towards an audience) was released. In Britain it sold miserably, but it was a different story in the States where, with the boast of their incessant gigging and heavy radio play, the album gave Humble Pie their first chart success, making Number 21.

'Rock On' was, though still flawed, a considerable improvement on its predecessor and while they were concentrating their line of attack to an entirely rock 'n' roll approach onstage, the music of 'Rock On' was as eclectic as that on 'Humble Pie', if not more so. The album's two weakest cuts were the out and out hard rockers 'Stone Cold Fever' and 'Rolling Stone', where the band lacked the finesse of Led Zeppelin to transform hard rock into something other than lumpen riffing. Frampton contributed the best song he'd written to date in the L.P.'s opening cut 'Shine On', a well constructed melodic rocker, pithy and with fine rock lyrics.

(Above) A refugee once more as Humble Pie reach their peak of acceptance with 'Rockin' The Fillmore'.

During 1971 Humble Pie played countless dates with those barons of mapcap heavy metal, Grand Funk Railroad, then one of America's biggest grossing (and grossest) rock acts. And their only British appearance all year was supporting Grand Funk at a free concert that summer in London's Hyde Park where the Pie actually received an ecstatic reception. Not long after the concert, Marriott told ''NME'', 'If we'd stayed in England we would have broken up because all it did was sap our confidence. We've realised that we're a good band and not a flash in the pan supergroup. We

had all that and it's taken us two years to live it down.'

He says, 'I left because I knew the live album was going to be a big album. It was at the same pitch I was just before I released 'Frampton Comes Alive'. It had got to the point where Humble Pie was doing what the audience wanted it to do and it was only one little stream of what it could do, I just couldn't see Humble Pie ever going back to being anywhere near an acoustic act. I was frustrated musically. Out of all the songs I was writing maybe one or two of them would suit Humble Pie When we formed Humble Pie we envis-

arrangement and the overall abundance of energy prove that on their night Humble Pie were as good as any other high energy rock band in the world. Frampton takes over the lime-light when he solos, which he often does; otherwise it's Marriott's show. True, the odd clichés creep into Frampton's playing now and then, but his playing on 'Rockin' The Fillmore' alone would have established his reputation as one of rock's finest guitarists. He isn't as tasteful as he would be on his solo albums, but his licks are charged with a hard rock power missing from 'Frampton Comes Alive'. There are not many rock guitarists who can sustain interest through several minute vamps and as 'Rockin' The Fillmore' shows, Peter Frampton is one of them.

FRAMPTON ANNOUNCED HIS DECISION TO split in late September, finally making up his mind while holidaying with Mary in Cyprus. As with his quitting The Herd, he'd taken the Big Step after mulling it over with the benefit of cool objectivity presented by a holiday. But this time, Frampton had made the decision entirely on his own with no Steve Marriott prompting him. Mary certainly didn't influence his decision and it's unlikely a dedicated musician like Frampton would ever make a major career decision because of anything a wife or girlfriend said. He has always put his career first and Mary says he's never had any doubts of his own ability to succeed, 'It's never been conceivable to him that he would never succeed,' she says. And while Frampton wasn't likely to starve (in April he'd bought a large house in London's St. John's Wood), seeing as how a man of his talents would always be in demand as a session player, he had finally put himself totally on the line.

Altham sees Frampton's quitting as a courageous act and one which Marriott resented, now that the group were on the eve of major success and would have to go to the trouble of finding a replacement. Wills, however, reckons Frampton would have been asked to leave the band if he'd stayed much longer simply because of the personality differences. He also says, 'If I didn't know him I'd never have understood why he left because to me Peter Frampton brought a touch of class to the band without any doubt at all. His guitar playing, those harmonies he used to do with Steve brought that little extra. They had a good tight unit but Peter's guitar playing always added a sparkle to the tracks.'

Marriott himself says he didn't resent Peter's leaving. Instead he says he was glad, 'We were very relieved. It obviously wasn't working. He was very ill. He was just eating that fucking cereal and nothing else. He didn't have it in him to do a strenuous rock 'n' roll show and because of it was screwing up the band's playing. It knackered him.'

Anthony thought Frampton's leaving was crazy, but he accepted it and calmly made the announcement to Yaskiel. Frampton had done what he had to do. And by doing it he would not only fulfil himself musically, but would also become a much happier person, not to mention a richer one. That's easy to say with hindsight. It was probably the last thing on Peter Frampton's mind when in late 1971 he pondered his future, still just 21 and already a refugee from two successful groups.

aged it being an extension of what the Small Faces had done on 'Ogden's Nut Gone Flake', but it wasn't. It could never be. We could never be the Small Faces.'

Released in November, 'Rockin' The Fillmore' did precisely what Frampton thought it would, quickly going gold in America and boosting the group to become over the next two years one of America's top live attractions. The album is patchy, but tracks like the blistering 'I Don't Need No Doctor' and 'Rolling Stone', which despite running for 16 minutes is compelling for Marriott's infectious vocals, the band's intelligent

"Is that what you feel about it? Do you think it's all bullshit?"

NOW THAT PETER FRAMPTON HAD ESTAB-lished a reputation as a guitarist of rare talent he had no trouble in finding good musicians to work with him. And amond the contributors to his first solo album 'Wind of Change', released April 1972, were Billy Preston, in his time keyboard player to the Beatles and the Rolling Stones, and Ringo Starr.

Frampton had experienced his first taste of working with a former Beatle the previous year when, after a chance meeting with George Harrison's assistant Terry Doran, a friend of Mary Frampton's, Peter played on Hari's 'All Things Must Pass' album. Recalls Mary, 'We were having a drink in the Chasse in Wardour Street and Terry said a friend of his was doing a session round the corner, why didn't Peter come down. Peter was knocked out at playing with George Harrison. They're both a bit introverted and at first were shy of each other.' An oversight on Harrison's part, however, meant that Peter Frampton's name wasn't listed among the record's credits, but he did invite Frampton to play the historic Concert for Bangla Desh at New York's Madison Square Garden in August 1971. Logistical problems intervened and Frampton didn't play the gig.

'Wind of Change' isn't a superstar-studded record; Ringo plays on two cuts while Preston's role is restricted to the closing 'Alright'. And for the majority of the tracks Frampton worked with his erstwhile colleague Andy Bown (keyboards and bass), drummer Mike Kellie, ex-Spooky Tooth, and bassist Rick Wills; Kellie and Wills were later to play in Frampton's Camel, Peter's first post-Humble Pie band. 'Wind of Change' is a remarkably mature first album with none of the teething problems associated with debut discs. With its well crafted songs, creative arrangements, stunning guitar work, excellent musicianship and production, 'Wind of Change' is far superior to Frampton's subsequent two solo albums. It wasn't until the 1975 release of 'Frampton', the album which finally captured the imagination of the American record-buying public picking Peter up from the doldrums and launching him into his trip to phenomenasville, that he came up with a record as good as this first one.

'Wind of Change' also gave Frampton the first opportunity in his career to flex his fingers at the studio board. And what a fine producer he is, working in cahoots with engineer Chris Kimsey with whom Frampton has continued to work till this day. Ever since he was a kid Frampton had been a gadget freak and in the studio he could let his passion run riot, as Rick Wills

points out: 'Chris is good at getting the sound Peter wants. Peter's a great fiddler. He'll spend hours just getting one drum sound. And Kimsey was into doing things like that whereas quite a lot of guys can't be bothered.'

While 'Wind Of Change' picked up unanimous critical approval, it wasn't a big seller — failing to chart on either side of the Atlantic. Frampton knew the only way he'd sell records was, like Humble Pie, to get out on the road and sell himself that way. There was passing talk of forming a superstar band, utilizing some of the musicians who'd worked on 'Wind Of Change', but Frampton being the sensible guy he undoubtedly is (such a band would have been short lived), choose to work with Wills, Kellie and keyboard player Mick Gallagher who'd worked with Wills in the past. That summer the group rehearsed in the Old Kent Road, and Kellie finally came up with the name Camel for the group. They wasted no time in trying to crack the British market, and in September Frampton's Camel hit the dollar trail. It was to be the first bout of four years of solid, dogged touring which at one point would almost break Frampton's resolve.

THERE'S A LOT OF IDLE TALK ABOUT DUES paying by rock musicians but from here on in Frampton would pay his dues in no uncertain terms — not that he'd been sitting on his butt in previous years. He'd already put in a fair amount of spade work with the Pie, now he was digging on his own, starting from rock bottom and playing anywhere he could. You name it, and if it's American and has a stage, Frampton has played it.

He told me, 'I was on call all the time, not to tour but to work constantly. Some of the dates didn't come in till three days beforehand. I needed a lot of work to bolster my confidence and learn to be a front-man, which I'd never been before.' Prior to leaving for the States, Frampton had finally married Mary Lovett on August 24. At the wedding reception Frampton played his guests Stevie Wonder's masterpiece, 'Music Of My Mind'. Frampton had recently been converted to the Motown star and soon Wonder became without question Frampton's favourite songwriter.

At first Frampton's Camel was playing anything from opening concerts at 10,000 seater stadiums to headlining tiny clubs. 'You name them, I've played with them,' he says. 'I've never played with the Eagles or the Beach Boys but I've played with every other

American band.' And a few British ones too, including Humble Pie who, with former Colosseum guitarist Clem Clemson replacing Frampton, were going from strength to proverbial strength on the American boards.

Frampton's Camel played their only British tour at the end of the year — supporting Humble Pie. Recalls Frampton, 'I did it to show there was no animosity between me and Steve. I was petrified 'cause Humble Pie was a machine by then. All the roadies were like computers and everything was very well worked out. And there was I with rented amplifiers and things tied together with string, not knowing which mike to sing into, having no balance and no arrangements worked out.'

Frampton also played numerous gigs in the States supporting Humble Pie where he could at first hand see the success he'd walked out on. Wills remembers, 'There was a cold war between Pete and Steve. They never tried to get back to being matey again. They've seen each other since. I know they talk to each other. Whatever Steve's into he's into it four hundred per cent and he just doesn't really take a lot of notice of what anybody else is doing. Pete took more notice of Humble Pie because we were always hearing about what the Pie had done, how they'd sold out here, how they'd sold out there, how they were using Lear Jets to fly everywhere.

'They were so big and we were playing the biggest places with them. We would go out and obviously try to do the best we could. We used to score well but when a band's that big there's no competition. It would be like someone now going on tour with Pete. You can't compete with that kind of audience reaction. Seeing the

Pie in the lap of luxury didn't make Pete regret his leaving them but there were slight pangs.'

On their return to England, Kellie had been dropped from the band by Frampton. Wills recalls, 'I don't think he was right for the band mentally or musically. He was into lots of excess. Pete just didn't want that getting in the way. Rather than put up with another hassle he didn't need, he thought it would be easier to get another drummer. I didn't think he'd be able to find another drummer to replace Kellie 'cause he had that deft sort of touch — not particularly heavy, but pushy.' Kellie's successor was former Motown sessioner John Siomos, a New Yorker who engineer Eddie Kramer had turned the band onto and who made his studio debut with Frampton on 'Frampton's Camel'. Recorded at the end of 1972 and released the following April, 'Frampton's Camel' wasn't a worthy successor to 'Wind Of Change'. Too many of the songs were all hook and no verses. There were exceptions like 'Lines On My Face' — as in all of Frampton's songs the lyrics were drawn from personal experience and his number referred to his rapidly deteriorating relationship with Mary — characterised by excellent reflective guitar as well as being a finely crafted song. 'White Sugar' was a good little rocker on which Frampton played, unusually enough, slide guitar. And the closing, lengthy group composition, 'Do You Feel Like We Do', was interesting with its insidious riff and looping guitar phrases, if a little short on pizzazz. Like 'Lines On My Face', 'Do You Feel Like We Do' would subsequently become a live tour de force. The number was sired during the band's initial rehearsals in the Old Kent Road.

'The words are pretty silly. There's lines in there I

very much doubt people would understand. All that stuff about white tails and top hats came from a photo session we did for A&M where we all wore evening dress. There's also a line in there about Kellie getting busted. Peter would usually lay a song on the band in the studio or at a rehearsal but that's an exception.

'He never told anyone what to play. He always used to like everyone's playing. That's why you become one of the band — for what you could do and not for what he could get out of you. The arrangements were invariably group arrangements. Before we put the vocals on, some of the things were amazing just as instrumentals 'cause I think he failed — he knows it as well — with lyrics. They're often bland. They're too personal. I used to be really disappointed sometimes with the final thing after hearing the backing tracks. He'd put a vocal on which should lift the song but it didn't. He can sing well but the way he writes lyrics makes it even more difficult for himself to sing. Whereas if he sings somebody else's song he usually sings it better.'

Rightly so, Frampton has often publicly criticized his powers as a lyricist. He told "Circus" in 1976, 'For me lyrics are the most difficult part of what I do. I can't fabricate them. I can't sing about something that I don't believe in or that hasn't happened to me. I used to hide meanings with little innuendoes, but now I think they're getting better. Listening to some of them now, they make me want to puke.'

Not only was Frampton's growing love for Stevie Wonder's music apparent on the Camel album in that it was a much more keyboard dominated record than its precursor, with far less emphasis on guitar, but side one closed with a less than wonderful version of Wonder's stirring love song from 'Talking Book': 'I Believe (When I Fall In Love With You It Will Be Forever)'. Frampton's vocals are pitifully histrionic as he tries too hard to pay homage to his idol. The band had bought 'Talking Book' the day they recorded the song and, says Wills, 'I Believe' cried out to be covered.

'Frampton's Camel' did nothing to hasten Frampton's rise to the top and he continued to slog at the American tour circuit, soon whittling away the money he'd earnt with Humble Pie by keeping Camel on the road. As Wills points out, he'd made his bed and now had no choice but to lie in it. 'He'd got the commitment, not only to himself but to the band and the advance the record company had put into him, so he was determined and obliged to make it to get these things straight. He'd take all the work he could get.'

Says Frampton, 'It wasn't the fact the music wasn't happening — it was. But the more you tour, the more you go in debt. And I would always pay my band, however meek the figure was, even if I couldn't pay myself. I always have more to lose, or more to make than them, but it got to the point where I couldn't move without asking the record company or Dee to go for more money. I had $70,000 from the record company advances that I put right in. As soon as that was gone Dee took over and was putting money in.'

Inevitably the name Camel was dropped, according to Wills at Dee Anthony's request, and the band now went out under Peter Frampton's name, something which didn't meet with the group's approval. Wills said, 'John thought it was another nail in the coffin for the band and it would end up with Peter getting everything. Pete used to always say if this band ever makes it I want you to feel an equal part of it and we'll split all the monies but it never really happened. I don't suppose it ever will. Pete made it as democratic as possible while realising it was him who was going to make it. Still, he was putting all the energy into it. He had a lot of energy. He'd never get cocky 'cause he can't do it. He hates that sort of thing. He was always easy to talk to about things. We used to discuss it but he didn't really know as much as he would have liked to know what was going on himself 'cause he felt frustrated by what was going on — basically he didn't know what he was supposed to be doing.

'He thought, 'Well I've been playing all these gigs, am I supposed to be . . . ?' He wanted some form of direction at that time. He was feeling a bit lost 'cause we were all turning to Pete and saying, 'What's happening, man?', looking for choice ways of getting there a bit quicker.'

While Humble Pie were being shipped around in limos, Frampton's band would be consistently broke, to the point of taking the booze the promoters had laid on for them at the gig back to their hotel because they couldn't afford to go out ligging. Most evenings they'd busy themselves jamming back in their hotel rooms which they'd share two a room. Wills remembers, 'We used to have quite a lot of fun with Peter. He's not a big raver. He doesn't drink a lot.' During a summer break in '73, Frampton asked Gallagher to leave the group. 'Peter decided he wasn't up to par musically,' says Wills. 'He didn't feel Mick was contributing much to the music. It was a very difficult decision to make because he was such a likeable person, very easy to get on with. It was a downer losing him.'

(Top left) At last a settled band for Frampton, left to right, Bob Mayo [keyboards], Stanley Sheldon [bass] and John Siomos [drums].

CONSEQUENTLY FRAMPTON'S THIRD POST-Humble Pie album 'Something's Happening' was recorded with the band as a three piece, Frampton himself playing keyboards apart from two cuts where ace session piano player Nicky Hopkins stepped in. Frampton had been knocked out by Led Zeppelin's then current album, 'House Of The Holy' and recording for 'Something's Happening' started at Headley Grange, a converted country house where Zeppelin had recently been working. The group had heard rumors of Zeppelin dabbling in black magic there and sure enough Frampton and his cohorts experienced a very strange sequence of events before finally giving up the ghost and returning to work at London's Olympic and Island studios. 'There was a strange feeling about the house as if it was haunted,' says Wills. 'We got there, set up our gear but for some weird reason the stuff wouldn't go down on tape. It just wasn't being recorded. We used to work all night. Mikes weren't working, heads on machines weren't working. We were there four or five days and eventually got four or five tracks down, but we only used one.'

'Something's Happening', released in April 1974, was a major departure for Frampton, albeit a temporary one, in that it showed Frampton coming on altogether tougher than on his previous two albums. He wasn't into writing hard rock riff songs, but much of the music on 'Something's Happening' is pithy, with abrasive and vigorous acoustic guitars layered over the rhythm section on the lines of Zeppelin cuts like 'That's The Way' from 'Led Zeppelin Three'. Zeppelin were clearly influencing Frampton's music at this time and his vocal phrasing even betrayed a hint of Robert Plant's vocal style on side one's 'Golden Goose', a title presumably referring to his days as a pin-up boy. Moreover, his guitar playing, while not forsaking its characteristic lyricism, did at times show his current infatuation with Zeppelin. On 'Golden Goose' his playing, with an emphasis on sustain, is similar to Jimmy Page's less frenzied hard rock licks. The group too were playing harder — and funkier — contributing to the overall feeling of urgency which dominated the album. While the playing is always good, the material was inconsistent, particularly side two's 'Magic Moon' and 'Sail Away' which closed the album on an uninspired note.

The title cut, the then ironic 'Something's Happening', which a year later would seem peculiarly apt, was a great song, full-bodied, rockin' and yet with the kind of insidious melody line the subsequent 'Frampton' album would be full of. Frampton's guitar on the track sounded actually angry, born out of frustration. Along with the L.P.'s opening 'Doobie Wah', which makes no bones about its debt to the Doobie Brothers (who Frampton and his colleagues were hearing a lot on American radio), 'Something's Happening' would become a live staple. With its rough edges and inspired chord progression, 'Doobie Wah' was a fine, solid rock song.

Clearly, as the music on 'Something's Happening' reflects, Frampton had a struggle on his hands. In Britain the album sold no more or less than its predecessors, but in the States it, in Frampton's words, 'painfully charted' for a couple of weeks, before vanishing to obscurity. 'It was 74 with an anchor,' jokes Wills. And the title track, released as a single, which Frampton so hoped would catapult him into the premier league, didn't happen. Frampton, always critical of his own work, didn't like the record, which had exhausted his supply of songs. 'I had eight songs for the album and we recorded eight songs, he says. 'Whereas on 'Frampton' I had 15 and we recorded only eleven.'

Frampton toyed with the idea of replacing Gallagher in the line-up with guitarist Frank Carillo who'd worked on 'Wind Of Change', but after some hesitation he invited his old friend from the Herd, Andy Bown, to join the group on keyboards. Originally Bown agreed to do just the one tour, or rather one series of dates, because Frampton was still taking what he could get, but Bown stayed with the band for a year. Says Wills, 'Andy knew everything about Pete. He knew all his weaknesses and strengths and vice versa so it was really good for Pete to have Andy in the band. He knew he had someone to bounce off as well as having some competition 'cause Andy can write songs and is a good player. He fitted in well. Everybody felt it was right for him to be in the band. And I also had a drinking partner.'

Matters, Bown or no Bown, had reached an all time low for Frampton when in November he returned to England to record again. He later told ''Sounds'', 'It just gets to the point where the business overrides the audience. There's a point where you have to keep on playing because you're still promoting yourself, you're still trying to build that following, but at $1500 a night you can't go on doing it without owing a lot of money, and the more money you owe, the more weight is on your head, therefore it becomes incredibly depressing.'

That summer Wills' wife had given birth to the couple's first baby. Three days later he left for another American tour on the condition he'd be back in six weeks.

Three months later he returned to his wife and baby. He says, 'I left the group twice on that tour but I couldn't get home. I couldn't get a ticket. We were being brought to live in New York for three months and we weren't working. I spent days and days in hotel rooms. Peter had rented a house in Upstate New York and he was living there with Mary so it was all right for him. Andy and his wife were there too staying with Peter, and John's a New Yorker anyway. No money was being sent home 'cause I couldn't get in touch with Dee. Peter was having no more luck than we were in getting in contact with Dee and he didn't know what the next step was.' Anthony was ill at the time.

Wills' growing frustrations with the seemingly stagnant situation exploded in November when the group were waiting to record. Frampton, Bown and Wills had travelled down to a remote part of England on the Gloucestershire/South Wales border to Clearwell Castle which had been shrewdly revibed to accommodate recording rock bands. With the use of a mobile recording unit, rock acts could not only record in the impressive building, they could also sleep and eat there. John Siomos hadn't yet arrived because of problems the Musicians' Union were giving him. And he was twice sent back from Heathrow Airport. Wills finds it impossible to lay down tracks without a drummer and he and Bown had been spending their evenings in the local pub getting well and truly oiled. Says Wills, 'There was nothing else to do and the pub stayed open until you had no money in your pockets.' After one of these drinking bouts, Wills and Bown returned to the Castle, and went to the bowels of the Castle where the playing part of the recording was taking place. Naturally the room was wired up to the mobile studio — where Frampton was in fact tinkering around. So he not only inadvertently heard Wills saying in no uncertain terms what he thought of the band's current situation, he also recorded it.

Wills continues the story, 'Peter came storming down the stairs and said, 'Is that what you feel about it? Do you think it's all bullshit?' I said I did.' 'Three days later Frampton called Wills and said he thought it would be best if he severed his connection with the band. 'I demanded the tape be erased,' says Wills, 'but he wouldn't have it. He was trying to defend something he knew was wrong.'

SUCH WAS FRAMPTON'S DEPRESSION AT THE time that he considered giving up his career as a soloist for the relatively easier life of a session musician. A&M were beginning to wonder if they hadn't been pumping good money after bad and Frampton was now in debt to the tune of a quarter of a million dollars. He later told "Circus", 'Frampton' was a last attempt. If that album hadn't made it, it would've been the end. There would have been no way to keep going. We'd hit rock bottom.'

On completing the album Frampton moved permanently to the States, back to the house in Upstate New York he'd been renting that year. A new love had

entered his life, Penny McCall, two years older than Frampton and a double-divorcée. Peter and Penny, who with their fine bone structure and perfect pin-up-picture smiles share a disarming facial similarity to one another, had met when she was married to a roadie. Love might have come knocking on Frampton's door, but money was still in short supply. Guitars and Revoxes had to be sold before his emigration and six months later there was often some uncertainty as to where the rent money was coming from. It wasn't unusual for Frampton to have to cash a ten dollar cheque for spending money.

Released in April, 1975 'Frampton' immediately received more American radio-play than its forerunners. Four of its cuts, 'Show Me The Way', 'Baby I Love Your Way', 'Money' and 'Nowhere's Too Far For My Baby' got repeated airings on the American airwaves, as the programmers recognized the highly insidious quality of these songs. After shooting off on a tangent with 'Something's Happening', Frampton was back on course, maximizing his talents so that the songs on 'Frampton' had a completeness lacking in much of his previous material.

'Frampton' isn't a great album, but with its mellow, balmy, romantic ambience redolent of the Nassau environment in which much of it had been written, it is difficult to resist. Frampton had wanted to make it a very personal record and while being unable to articulate anything but the most prosaic statements on life and love 'Frampton' succeeds in communicating a certain warmth. Peter's guitar playing is as excellent as ever, introducing the talkbox guitar on 'Show Me The Way', a memorable song with a perfectly resolved melody which would a year later give Frampton a huge hit in Britain and America. If there were influences lurking in Peter Frampton's mind when he wrote these songs they're impossible to detect — apart from the closing 'Money', a grinding hard-rock riff song consciously written in the vein of Led Zeppelin. Otherwise the material on 'Frampton' possesses a refreshing originality.

Once again produced by Frampton and Kimsey, the sound on the record is remarkable, possessing as it does a disarming polished amateurish quality. So many contemporary rock records sound the same with their smug technical perfection, so 'Frampton' comes on like the proverbial shaft of sunlight.

While it didn't uncork the champagne bottle of American success, it put the glasses on the table and it wouldn't be long before Frampton was drinking draughts more voluptuous than anyone including his mum ever imagined. 'Frampton' just about nudged the American Top Twenty Album Charts and up until the release of 'Frampton Comes Alive' the following January had sold reasonably well, clocking up about 300,000 American sales.

FRAMPTON'S REAL STRENGTH, (SAID WITH the benefit of hindsight), is not in the studio but onstage, and with Anthony lavishing his attentions on Frampton, suggesting how he should pace his set, and use his face, body and voice to seize an audience's attention, it was only a matter of time before Peter Frampton bowled the collective American rock audience over.

Admits Frampton, 'Dee tutored me a lot in audience control, to act a song rather than just sing it.' He'd found the perfect band in Siomos, with bassist Stanley Sheldon replacing Bown, who even though he knew things were taking off wanted to go back to pursuing a solo career. Bob Mayo, formerly with Frank Carillos's group, was on keyboards and guitar, playing his mixture of pretty acoustic songs, rock and funk.

And with his overt vulnerability and accessability on stage, Peter Frampton soon began to wow guitar freaks, music freaks and boppers alike to the extent that in America's bicentenial year England not only distinguished itself as a country beleaguered by dought and wallowing in national debt, but also — to several million young Americans — as the birth place of one Peter Frampton. The man who came alive.

Epilogue

SO HOW DO YOU FOLLOW A 13 MILLION selling album? Quite simply you don't. And when at the beginning of June this year Frampton released "I'm In You", his first studio album in two years and almost 18 months after "Frampton Comes Alive" hit the shops, you'd never know from the music that it was the work of America's most popular rock star.

True, there were cameo appearances from Mick Jagger and Frampton's mainman (or should I say hero?) Stevie Wonder dropped in to blow harp on a song about Frampton's dog "Rocky's Hot Club" (well Neil Young wrote a song about his dog . . .), but "I'm In You" showed none of the signs of hyper-stardom, be they peerless excellence, an attempt to repeat former glories or just being well and truly pooped.

That said, "I'm In You", despite several moments of genuinely inspired music making, failed to either build on or repeat the organic ebullience of "Frampton", and didn't deserve to sell the million or so it did in its first week of release in America; as I write "I'm In You" (album) is poised to top the American charts and the single of the same name isn't far behind, but then when did deserving ever have anything to do with selling records?

Doubtless afraid to spend too much time in Britain for fear of being clobbered by that ubiquitous bogeyman, the British Inland Revenue (Frampton made a brief excursion to England in June to attend his brother's graduation ceremony), "I'm In You" was recorded at New York's "Electric Ladyland" studios, scene of the "Frampton's Camel" album four years previous. This time, though, Frampton's presence demanded the company of a clutch of bodyguards to ensure sessions weren't disrupted by overzealous Frampton Fans.

Working alongside Frampton in Electric Ladyland was Mick Jagger, presumably mixing the long overdue live Stones' double album, and as fate would have it Jagger pouted in one night and laid down a back-up vocal on the only goodish Frampton song on the entire album, "Tried To Love". Elsewhere Frampton's

songs are not only lyrically banal but the bulk of them lack a decent chord progression or an inspired arrangement; the title cut, a mawkish ballad of the tritest proportions dedicated to Peter's amour Penny, with whom he has recently split from, albeit on an amicable basis and with the view to future reconciliation, is pure MOR.

And even the well intentioned "Won't You Be My

Friend", a tribute to Frampton and his band's faves, the excellent Little Feat, doesn't have the necessary stuffing to carry it. Likewise the remainder of side one, "(Putting My) Heart On The Line" (what, again?) and "St Thomas (Don't You Know How I Feel)" (now doesn't that ring a bell?), are flimsy compositions.

"Tried To Love" is another plate of scollops, however, Frampton once again demonstrating his ability to write well constructed, melodic and catchy pop-rock tunes. In terms of arrangement, it's imaginative and Frampton wastes no time in playing exemplary guitar. El Feat's drummer Ritchie Hayward sits in to beef things up.

The following "Rocky's Hot Club" is a cute little novelty song and if any proof were needed of the excellence of Frampton's band, they play great on enthusiastic if not miraculous versions of two old Motown chestnuts, "(I'm A) Road Runner" and "Signed Sealed Delivered (I'm Yours)", perhaps a sign of Frampton having difficulty coming up with new material of his own, bassist Stanley Sheldon in particular performing with considerable aplomb.

By the time this reaches you "I'm In You" will no doubt have increased its sales fourfold.

If Frampton's status isn't apparent from the music itself, the marketing is a give-away, leaving nothing to chance in the Peter Frampton As Pop Star stakes. And those reading the sleeve carefully would find that they could now spend their dollars on Peter Frampton merchandise, all of which smacks of The Herd days and leads to speculation that Peter Frampton, despite his musical abilities and oft-stated desire to remain otherwise, has turned full circle and become a full blown pop star (again).

July 1977

Acknowledgements

A PART FROM WISHING TO THANK ALL THOSE people who allowed themselves to be interviewed for this book, special thanks to Kit Bucker at A&M Records, Roy Carr ("New Musical Express") and Chris Welch ("Melody Maker") for their help and encouragement. Special thanks, too, to Mr. & Mrs. Owen Frampton for their invaluable help in providing research material.

Photographers' Credits: Paul Canty, Page 5; André Csillag, 61; Robert Ellis, 38, 62; H. Goodwin, 18, 21, 22; Chris Holder, 47, 54, 59; London Features International, 51; Barry Plummer, 51, 52, 53; Napier Russell, 30; SKR, 36, 37, 43, 44, 46, 49; Pennie Smith, 3, 58, 62, 64; Chris Walker, 42, 61; George Wilkes, 34, 41.